JESUS, INC.

JESUS, INC.

THE VISIONARY PATH

AN ENTREPRENEUR'S GUIDE TO TRUE SUCCESS

LAURIE BETH JONES

CROWN
BUSINESS
NEW YORK

Published by Crown Business, New York, New York. Member of the Crown Publishing Group.

Random House, Inc. New York, Toronto, London, Sydney, Auckland
www.randomhouse.com

CROWN BUSINESS and colophon are trademarks of Random House, Inc.

Printed in the United States of America

Design by Susan Maksuta

Library of Congress Cataloging-in-Publication Data
Jones, Laurie Beth.
Jesus, Inc. : the visionary path : an entrepreneur's guide to true success /
by Laurie Beth Jones.
1. Management—Religious aspects—Christianity.   2. Success in business.
3. Jesus Christ—Leadership.   4. Executive ability—Biblical teaching.
I. Title.
HD38 .J6384 2001
658.4'21—dc21
00-064332

ISBN 0-609-60717-0

10 9 8 7 6 5 4 3 2 1

First Edition

To Linda Sterrett Marple,
my curly-headed friend,
who has stood with me
in darkness and in light.
And to her mother,
Jan Sterrett,
whose words of blessing
and challenge are finally coming true.

CONTENTS

Section Two

The Lurch: The Early Days and Your New Identity   71

Section Three

The Lessons: Learning Through the Wisdom and Mistakes of Others   143

ACKNOWLEDGMENTS

I want to thank Mary Ann Naples, my agent, for constantly encouraging me to sustain the creative tension of writing about spirituality in business. She was one of the first and most ardent champions for *Jesus, CEO*, and remains a light on my path to this day. I knew writing *Jesus, Inc.* was going to be a fun journey when I first met Bob Mecoy, my editor, whistling and half skipping down the hall to meet me. Thank you, Bob, for offering detailed examples and specific suggestions for improvement, rather than circling ten pages at a time with the single inked-in comment "Explain."

Mike Regan, my "CEO brother," checks in on me almost daily to see how I am doing, regardless of the multiple million-dollar business deals he has sitting on his desk. He has shown unfailing faith and discernment in helping guide me through business challenges and opportunities, and also stood knee-deep in mud to help deliver my first newborn colt. Rosario "Cha Cha" Munoz came out of an idyllic golfing retirement to help answer phones and sort files and unpack boxes and do whatever else is required. To Ron Lush and the Global Initiatives group in Phoenix, thank you for walking alongside me, and living your mission, which is "to serve leaders, and equip leaders to serve." Dave Cowan and Susanna Palomares continue to provide an idyllic writing environment for me, and demonstrate the gift of hospitality with such graciousness that I often feel like I have ascended into heaven in their presence. Thank you also to the people of Fourth Lake Community in the Adirondacks, for demonstrating how beautiful it is for people to dwell together in harmony.

I would also like to thank Will Weisser, Dorianne Steele, and Rhoda Dunn at Crown for their excellent and creative help.

To Doug Hawthorne, George Longshore, Peter Giammalvo, Marty Blubaugh, Greg Bunch, Billy Bob Harris, Debbie Bartlett, George Hester, Bonnie Dawson, Jess and Adrie Schulz, David Bach, Greg Bunch, Patrick Berry, Ken Blanchard, Sheldon Bowles, Bill Pollard, Bob Buford, Gene and Nancy Bradley, Jerry Mabe, Lee Ellis, Don Jacobson, Sue Clark, Leland and Lareeta Boren, Dee and Adair Margo, Steve Shull, Frank Mallinder, Jim Stanley, Kati Gerdau, John Pearson, Nicole Johnson, Rita Esparza-Flores, Dr. Dorothy Gault, Tom Heck, George Babbish, Daryl Travis, Roger Hawkins, John Brooks, Bill and Grace Nelson, Doug Coe, Dee Jones, Kathryn Antonacci, Ed Blitz, Kingsley Fletcher, and others—thank you for helping make my journey so interesting and exciting.

Others I'd like to thank include Richard Stenbakken, Misty Strawser, Gerry Wakeland, Gabrelle Kaniger, Betty Ann Bird, Rick and Randy Altig, Cinda Kinsey, James Stephens, Mitch Speed, Sister Marie Bush, Cherle Chartier Whiting, Shauna Volimer, Beverly Sanders, Ernest Fitzpatrick, Mike Mann, Dr. Walt Kallestad, Ron Mannix, Kristine Hartland, Duane Krueger, Lin Reams, Florence Pert, Dr. Arthur Calliandro, Rohn Ritzema, Jerry Brummitt, Elaine Winter, Lisa Dahlberg, Paula Stevenson, Gwinn Magee, Fred Roach, Boone Powell, Jr., Mary Graham, Steve Arterburn, Wendy Craig-Purcell, Beth

O'Dower, Michael Cardone, Jr., Rev. Howard Eddington, Odile Nicolette, Arlan Fuhr, DC, Franklin Beach, Judy Budd, Rev. M. De Chantal St, Howard Good, Joe Tye, Tammy Czyzewski, Bill and Gloria Gaither, Andrew Colyer, Dennis Griffith, Lawrence Kent, Hal Anderson, Sandra Foyil, Ed McLaughlin, Judy Taylor, Ron Gladden, Kathy Berggren, Ray and Karen Hruby, Elaine Winter, Gwinn Magee, Bill Watson, Mary Omwake, Tim Garrison, Brad Lindemann, David Nicely, Charles Waldo, Carol Samuelson, Terri Elton, Cathy Trame, Marisa Merritt, David Gjosund, Ann Zimmerman, Sandra Ward, Hugh Hodge, Kathy Fife, Maggie Moody, Marsha Casey, David Butler, Kevin Campbell, Carol Schneider, Norma Smoker, Mario Barnabe, George and Marylss Carolson, Robert Pinhero, Kianta Prince Bryant, and others for enlisting me to speak to your co-workers and friends. Blessings to you all!

For laughter, love, and light I want to thank my family, Kathy, Ben, Benny, Wade and Tara Ivey, Joe Jones and Barbara Hanlon, as well as Irene, Ricardo, Joseph and Jacob Pratt, and Yvonne, Miguel, Gabriela, and Antonio Gomez. Thank you, Tara, especially, for helping so much with this manuscript, and doing so in a way that made it all seem so easy. For constant encouragement and an example of what Christianity really means, I want to thank Irma Soto. Her dedication to serving the church and the poor are a humbling reminder to me of God's most precious priorities.

My mother, Irene Jones, encourages me to live my dream by continuing to live hers. Catherine Calhoun keeps me laughing when I feel like crying, and quickly gets to the heart of the matter when I fly all around it.

To my Path facilitators, thank you for your commitment to helping others find their Path. I pray God's blessing on you all.

INTRODUCTION

A NEW MODEL

In the last few years, I have become aware of a new breed of businesspeople. I call them spiritreneurs (spirit-ra-nurs).

"Spiritreneur" is derived from the words *spirit* and *entrepreneur*. *Webster's Dictionary* defines spirit briefly as "the soul or heart, as the seat of feelings" and entrepreneur as "a person who organizes and manages an enterprise, especially a business, usually with considerable initiative and risk." Thus, spiritreneurs are those who fully integrate their soul in a workplace enterprise. If you want to know whether or not *you* are a spiritreneur, just ask yourself two questions. "Would I be doing this work even if I weren't getting paid?" and "Am I doing this work as unto the Lord?" If your answer to both of these questions is yes, you are on your way to "spiritreneurship."

Spiritreneurs are springing up all over. Never before have so many people been willing, and able, to launch endeavors that reflect not only their highest gifts and beliefs but also benefit others while doing so.

In preparing for this book I asked a number of spiritreneurs to share with me their greatest concerns. Among them were:

1) Being able to honor God continuously in their work
2) Being able to discern God's will on a daily basis
3) Being perceived as credible in the marketplace

They also shared with me the ups and downs, the swamps and meadows, the tremendous variety of spiritual landscapes that they have encountered while attempting to integrate God fully into their work life. As a vice president of Service Master, a multibillion-dollar company, shared in a recent group forum, "Our mission is to honor God, develop people, pursue excellence, and create profits. I guarantee I haven't seen a day yet where all four were happening simultaneously."

Yet it is possible to have the combination. Never before have people had the opportunity and ability to do what they love and be supported economically while doing so. No longer do you have to enter the ministry, per se, to be able to give glory to God. This book is about that phenomenon. And it is based on the life of a man I call the original spiritreneur.

Let's look for a moment at Jesus of Nazareth. He had a good job. A solid job. He had taken over his father's business after his death, and he enjoyed what he did. Working with wood was satisfying to him. He seemed to have a knack for repairing things as well as fashioning new designs for chairs and tables. His customers counted on him to build things that would last. But there was a restlessness inside he couldn't deny. It had been growing in him for years, in fact. As much as he enjoyed working with wood, he loved working with people more. And one day—which was an accumulation of days, really, and nights of waking in his room, praying that God would give him guidance—he told his mother that he was going to leave. In what must have been a dramatic moment he turned over the key to his carpentry shop and walked out the door.

Jesus, as unique as he was, was also like so many of us who are engaged in one kind of work yet yearn to be doing another. Jesus was a true spiritreneur—perhaps the ultimate spiritreneur—because he created a new category of work for himself and was able to make a living doing what he most loved. Yes, it was his Father's will. But it was his will, too. And he was economically sustained and supported as he went about his Father's work.

We don't know, exactly, how Jesus got paid. There is some understanding that he was supported by a group of wealthy women—sponsors, if you will, who believed in his work. When he had transportation needs he had an incredible network of friends and angels who saw to it that he never walked unless he wanted to. He got lots of free meals, being regularly invited to dine with some of the wealthiest people in the region. The fact that he brought along his twelve friends was a bit annoying, perhaps, but the hosts always managed to make room for them all. Sometimes it got even more complicated, like the time when a group of Jesus fans knocked a hole in the roof to lower a sick person down in front of Jesus. Judas probably took care of the expenses that time, although he wasn't happy about it.

In the sudden rush of customer demand, a small matter of paying Jesus' taxes was overlooked. Matthew, who had been a tax collector before he became a spiritreneur, knew how serious an offense that was. Yet Jesus simply told his team to go get the money from his offshore account—which at the time consisted of a coin in a fish's mouth.

From a distance we might say Jesus had it easy, having a rich Dad and all. But he, too, experienced hunger and frustration when the customers weren't accepting his offer, especially when they claimed not even to understand it. In fact, he couldn't give the Gift away free to most of his target customer base. And then there were the jealous "competitors" who were always following him, trying to make him look bad—jumping on everything he said in an effort to discredit him.

But Jesus was a spiritreneur in that he wanted more than anything to do what he came to do, and he wanted more than anything for others to have an abundant life as well. That is why he called out "Follow me!" to a group of people who already had steady, well-paying jobs. He said (in essence), "There is work to be done that will give you greater joy than you have ever known. You will rise each day eager to greet the dawn. You will learn to overcome your fears. And instead of just Caesar's coins filling your pockets your heart will overflow. I guarantee it with my life."

Jesus was a spiritreneur. He fully integrated his spiritual gifts and his daily work, and he made a living doing it. How exciting to be able to hear his call and follow his example—to use our talents to help others, and ascend to God in the process.

WHERE THEY'RE COMING FROM

The climate in which today's spiritreneurs are budding has been created by the convergence of four streams of events.

The first stream, called downsizing, began as a trickle from the Fortune 500 corporations. In the late 1980s and early '90s, these lumbering entities suddenly found they had too many workers with not enough to do. So they threw them out the window, and the bodies began to float downstream. The people thrown out the window weren't bad or incompetent or people who had made mistakes on the job. They were just "extra" people, labeled by cost-cutting accountants looking at things called the "bottom line" and "increasing shareholder value." The message to those standing on the banks was clear. You can't count on big companies to always give you a job.

The second stream was dissatisfaction—the dissatisfaction of aging baby boomers who began to say, "Why am I working in the first place? What does this work mean in terms of making the world better?" People decided that they weren't willing to toe the corporate line or exchange their souls for a paycheck anymore. People were looking for significance, not just success.

The third stream was technology. The Internet was born. The Internet, fax machines, phones that didn't have to be plugged into walls, and a dozen other new contact and communication devices awakened people to the possibility that maybe, just maybe, they didn't have to work downtown or drive all the way to the office so they could be present at corporate headquarters. Maybe they could work at home and still engage in commerce with anyone, anywhere.

The fourth stream is called the expectation of the new economy. *Fast Company* magazine sums it up by saying, "But the new economy [has never been] about a guarantee, whether in the form of ever-rising stock prices or of uniformly virtuous leaders. It was always (and still is) about a promise. The promise that you could combine a thirst for competition with a commitment to making a social contribution. The promise that you could do great work—and do work that matters to you. In other words, the promise that you could create wealth and live by values that you are proud of."

The result of these four streams converging has created a huge river of spiritreneurs—people who want to contribute their unique business gifts, ideas, and passion to the world in a way that is socially significant. Many people now truly believe that *work is love made visible,* and want to act on their beliefs.

DO YOU WANT A JOB OR A MISSION?

Numerous career planners and executive placement consultants are predicting that "jobs" will soon be a thing of the past—that in the near future, people will be defined by their mission, not their job descriptions. While at one time people had limited choices of what to do with their lives, the options are now wide open.

Ed Blitz is a financial planner who exudes wisdom and kindness as he dispenses "dollarly" advice. One client of his told me, "If Ed weren't an accountant, he'd be a rabbi." Ed decided early on that helping people with their financial needs was an incredible way to serve them. In addition to handling some of the wealthiest individuals and largest firms in Southern California, Ed also writes a newspaper column for kids, designed to help them learn about money. He has written a book that he gives to his clients, *The 10% Solution,* urging them to save, save, save. He loves his work, he loves his clients, and they love him. He drives a little blue BMW home at night, happy, knowing that today he made a difference in the lives of his clients—or perhaps in the life of a child he may never meet. Ed Blitz is a spiritreneur.

Thomas S. Monaghan, the founder of Domino's Pizza, recently sold his shares for one billion dollars so that he could be totally free to give it away. He now busies himself full-time working with Catholic Charities. Thomas Monaghan has become a spiritreneur.

Two women friends, meeting for lunch regularly in New York City, found themselves talking about the stresses of their jobs. Susan was a senior editor at one of the most successful magazines in the world. Angela was a publicist with one of the largest public relations agencies in the country. Both of them admitted to being dissatisfied with what they were doing. Despite the security and success they had attained in their careers, they felt there was something more. They read *The Path* and several other books that helped crystallize their new mission. They decided to quit their jobs and create something new—a public relations agency specializing in promoting people with messages of significance. Susan and Angela have become spiritreneurs.

Six months ago I had lunch with the CEO of a manufacturing company which last year grossed $4 billion in sales. Over chicken salad we shared our various journeys and looked toward the future. I asked him what he saw for himself in the next few years. He got tears in his eyes and then said, "To tell you the truth, I want to be doing what you're doing—helping release spirituality in the world." In a few years when he leaves his current duties and become an itinerant speaker, I will rejoice because he is following his dream. He is becoming a spiritreneur.

Jesus said, "You must be born again in order to enter the Kingdom of Heaven." By this he meant that you had to be born once to the world, and once again to the knowledge of God through him. I have come to believe that we now must be born three times—once to the world, once to God, and once to ourselves. Because only when we can see who we are and what we stand for—what we want to be about in the world—does every action we take suddenly seem significant. That is the point at which we have realized a vision of ourselves and our path through this world—a path that defines true success.

MY EXPERIENCE

My mother exhorted all of us children never to lead "lives of quiet desperation." I remember determining at an early age that the one word I hated almost more than any other was *mediocre.* I never wanted to live a boring life. Yet I too was drawn into the stream of the current thinking of my peers, which dictated an early marriage and trying to become materially successful. It worked for a while. I went to the seminars and read all the books and did what the experts said I should do, yet found myself, at the age of forty, divorced with crushing chest pains and shooting pains down my left arm. I watched in dismay as my two-year-old mini–real estate empire in California began to crumble, and, due largely to the ensuing recession, my advertising clients also began to disappear.

That is when I turned back to God. It was in this wilderness that I looked again at what I really wanted to be about. I assessed what my divine gifts were, and resolved to use them to make a difference, no matter what the cost. It was too painful to do otherwise. I wrote a book called *Jesus, CEO,* and my life took a new direction. Without my fully recognizing it, I had become a spiritreneur.

THE TIME IS RIGHT

Where once Paul had to earn a living making tents so that he could then go out and preach, now Paul could combine his preaching and his tent making into one company. Tom's of Maine or Land's End or Ben & Jerry's are examples of huge, multimillion-dollar companies using their position and their profits to promote goodness in the world.

Among the most interesting phenomena present in the current business climate are companies that have decided that part of doing well is doing *good.* This is even true in the Internet sector, where a number of companies have set aside shares in their initial public offerings (IPOs) for charities. Steve Kirsch, founder of Infoseek, has formed a new company called Propel. Backers include Intel CEO Andy Grove, Netscape founder Marc Andreessen, Dell founder Michael Dell, and eBay CEO Meg Whitman. All have pledged to donate a portion of Propel's market value to charity.

Likewise, Pierre Omidyar, founder of eBay, is now fostering a network of "social entrepreneurs" who intend to reinvent charity. Like a venture capital firm, this group is seeding a number of small causes in a style that has come to be called "venture philanthropy." They give money to charities that follow solid business plans and create earnings streams that sustain the nonprofit work.

Bill Ford Jr., the new head of Ford Motors, says, "This company will do best for its shareholders if it takes care of its employees, its community, and the environment. This will enable Ford Motors to attract better talent, develop loyal customers, enhance its brand, sell more cars and services, and, over time, boost its share price." You can see evidence of spiritreneurism in companies around the world. This idea of doing well by doing right is becoming so pervasive that to many folks it just seems like good business.

THE ENTREPRENEURIAL MINDSET

Few joys are comparable to that of launching and building your own business. I believe it so strongly that I think there should be courses on entrepreneurship starting at the grade-school level. As my friend and mentor Catherine Calhoun used to say, "Having your own business is the one area in your life—and perhaps the only area in your life—where you can experience the joy of directing your own destiny."

As I read the letters I've received since I began writing, I've recognized a yearning that so many of us have. The yearning is to dedicate our talents and gifts to some form of good-multiplying enterprise that not only nourishes our soul but feeds others on a daily basis.

What keeps us from it? One drawback is that many people still believe that God and business have nothing in common. People who are spiritually motivated have often felt guilt or shame about trying to earn a profit. What they overlook is the parable Jesus told about the master who gives three servants varying amounts of money *(talents)* before setting off on a journey:

To one he gave five talents, to another two, to a third one, one—
each in proportion to his ability. Then he set out on his journey.
The man who had received five talents promptly went and traded
with them and made five more. The man who had received two
made two more in the same way. But the man who received one
went off and dug a hole in the ground and hid his master's
money. Now, a long time afterward, the master of those servants
came back and went through his accounts with them. The man
who had received the five talents came forward bringing five
more. "Sir," he said, "you entrusted me with five talents and here
are the five more that I have made." His master said to him,
"Well done, good and trustworthy servant, you have shown you
are trustworthy in small things; I will now entrust you with
greater; come and join your master's happiness." He did likewise
with the man with the two talents. However, last came forward
the man who had the single talent. "Sir," said he, "I had heard
you were a hard man, reaping where you had not sown and
gathering where you had not scattered; so I was afraid, and I
went off and hid your talent in the ground. Here it is; it was
yours, you can have it back." But his master answered him, "You

unworthy and lazy servant! So you knew that I reap where I have not sown and gather where I have not scattered? Well, then you should have deposited my money with bankers, and on my return I would have got my money back with interest. Now take the talent from him and give it to the man who has the ten talents, for everyone who has, will be given more, and those who have not, will be deprived even of what he has. As for this good for nothing servant, throw him into the darkness outside, where there will be weeping and grinding of teeth."
(Matthew 25:14–30)

Jesus here clearly displays an appreciation for business principles properly applied. The "good and trustworthy servant" is the one who traded with his talents, and increased them. He is the one who entered into his master's happiness, and was given even more talents to oversee. The servant who claimed to know his master as a hard man ended up with nothing. He buried the one talent he was given, in fear that he would lose even that, and in the end lost not only the talent but the approval of his master.

Not too long ago I was asked to speak at a Christian college in a small town in Indiana. I discovered that students who chose to major in business constantly had to justify their choice to the other students who had chosen majors such as church leadership or social work. The business majors were made to feel guilty for wanting to pursue a calling in business. It was as if many doubted that these young people could follow this path and still remain Christian. I reassured them that it is indeed possible. That it is, in fact, necessary for people with spiritual values to express their talents in the business world.

THE SEVEN GIFTS OF BUSINESS

I believe the business world is the most exciting "mission field" that exists today. Where else do people spend the bulk of their time and energy? At its best, business offers us seven gifts:

1. *Dignity.* The ability to create jobs that give people a sense of dignity and purpose, as well as a reason to get up in the morning, is one of the most important offerings of business.

2. *Acknowledgment.* Businesses ideally create an atmosphere where the gifts and talents of the people within them are recognized and rewarded. This recognition encourages people to grow.

3. *Prosperity.* Business helps create abundance for entire communities, bringing new levels of activity and prosperity to entire groups of people. If you've ever driven through a ghost town, you will recognize that where there is no commerce, entire communities dry up and die.

4. *Integrity.* Businesses can survive only if they create value and deliver goods and services as promised, on time.

5. *Service.* Businesses must constantly evaluate how they treat their customers. Successful businesses have a culture of service and respect that can elevate the self-esteem of everyone they encounter.

6. *Community.* Businesses create a community where people interact, and get to know and care for one another. In many instances, the workplace has become the village.

7. *Challenge.* Businesses constantly challenge people to stretch emotionally, intellectually, and spiritually, learning as they grow.

As children many of us were eager to open lemonade stands or sell apples from our little red wagons door to door, but somehow that creative, entrepreneurial spirit gets hammered out of us. We begin to look to a single source of income—first to Mom and Dad's wallet and later on to huge corporations. The entrepreneurial spirit is, more than anything else, a way of looking at the world—of seeing opportunities instead of obstacles, of believing that money can be found in many different places, in many different ways. Too many of us are trained to be oxen, treading the rows that are laid out before us, adjusting uneasily but inevitably to the harness which is given to us to plow someone else's field, earning a bit of grain and hay at the end of the day.

Spiritreneurs don't mind plowing, but it will be new fields that we plow. Spiritreneurs find ways to integrate our spiritual lives with our work lives in exciting enterprises, and in doing so become the most fulfilled and happiest workers on the planet.

THE DOWNSIDE OF BUSINESS

There are more than sixteen million small business owners in the United States, most of whom began their businesses with dreams of increased freedom, autonomy, and wealth. Every 24 hours, 1,600 women launch their own companies, many of them on a wing and prayer. But over 80 percent of small businesses fail within the first five years. As Michael Gerber pointed out in his seminal book, *The E Myth,* many entrepreneurs are unprepared for the emotional toll their businesses command. Some fail to see that their enterprises, which were initially designed to support them, can slowly suffocate them with their demands.

Business at its worst represents a false, all-consuming god that demands your time, talents, and energy yet leaves you depleted, discouraged, and distanced from all that really matters. The same Jesus who told the story of rewarding workers who multiplied what they had been given warned that it is easier for a camel to go through the eye of a needle than for a rich man to enter heaven. He also said, "Where is the profit if you gain the whole world, yet lose your own soul?" (Mark 8:36).

Spiritreneurs deal with this tension daily. We employ gifts that can be used for good or ill. Yet we willfully choose to follow the path that Jesus has shown us, hoping to do well by doing right, and therein finding our blessing.

Jesus, Inc. addresses the opportunities and problems of spiritreneurship from a practical and spiritual point of view. By combining real-life stories and biblical principles, I hope to encourage and prepare you for the battles that lie ahead.

The book is divided into what I call The Four Phases of Spiritreneurship:

1. The Launch: Heeding the Call to Spiritreneurship
2. The Lurch: The Early Days and Your New Identity
3. The Lessons: Learning Through the Wisdom and Mistakes of Others
4. The Love: Living the Visionary Life of the Spiritreneur

What I hope is that you will learn how to harness that initial upsurge of inspiration and make it last. And, when you find yourself bogged down in a swamp of inertia and indecision, that the tools you'll find here will help you get yourself up and out. Here, those who encounter relationship challenges at work and home will learn to utilize more effective routes of communication and navigation. And all of us will be reminded that the be-all and end-all of any truly successful spiritreneur's work is love—the kind of love that transcends all toil, all tears, and all time.

JESUS, INC.

THE LAUNCH: HEEDING THE CALL TO SPIRITRENEURSHIP

I stood before 250 business leaders who had gathered in a palace in Austria for a special summit on Innovative Leadership and asked them one simple question. "What percentage of people would you estimate are in the wrong jobs?" Their almost unanimous response was "seventy percent."

There was then a long silence as we all contemplated the implications of it. If indeed what these business leaders believe is true, that seven out of ten people are working in the wrong jobs, then putting those people in the right positions could improve productivity, morale, performance, and profitability, which is every business leader's ultimate goal.

Let me ask you a question: Which musical note is a wrong note? Is B-flat a wrong note? C sharp? Obviously, there are no "wrong" musical notes, but only notes that are in the wrong place at the wrong time, thus destroying the harmony. I believe that Heaven will consist of every person doing what s/he most loves—of every note being in its right place. To me, Hell will be an eternity of people having to do work they hate.

Perhaps you are one of those people. You want desperately to express your talents, but you've been stuck in the wrong seat and given the wrong instrument in the orchestra. Perhaps you are feeling guilty about your lackluster performance. Maybe you are feeling angry and are not exactly sure where to direct your frustration. Or, perhaps you are hearing sounds that indicate you need to be doing something else, but are not sure exactly where those sounds are coming from, or why.

Those sounds may be your future calling, may be your call to spiritreneurship. "The Launch" will offer you practical examples of how to discern what is in your heart, and thus, your future. Maybe you are feeling the first tickle of wing feathers beneath your clothes. Maybe, like Gideon, you are hiding in a low-level job, thinking God can't find you there. Maybe you are a widow, in the sense that you have lost your former identity, either through downsizing or retirement or death of a loved one. God has a message for you, and it's good. Read these pages, and think about the words of Jesus, the world's most original spiritreneur. And remember always what he taught us, "With God, nothing is impossible."

HE BELIEVED HE COULD FLY

Riding one of the winged creatures, he flew.

—2 Samuel 22:11

For each spiritreneur there is a moment when the lights go on—when every cell in the body seems to shout, "I can fly!"

Fly where? Fly when? Fly how? Fly with whom? These must all be predicated by the very first question, which is: "Why fly?"

The answer is: "Because you can." Every single human being is capable of soaring beyond the daily grind and experiencing the bliss of heavenly support and motion.

Spiritreneurs are those who bring their heart and mind and soul and strength—fully integrated—into the work they do, and they do their work to honor God. Therefore, a waiter who makes his guests feel like kings and queens can be just as much a spiritreneur as the housewife who decides to start selling baskets out of her home so she can spend more time with her children.

3

I met a spiritreneur recently when I was on a speaking engagement at Lake Tahoe. The shuttle driver, Ron, met me at the gate with a hand-lettered sign with my name on it. He smiled and said, "I'll be your chauffeur for the evening." He gathered my luggage and, whistling softly, loaded it up. He got out a small step stool to help me up into the large van and then we began our journey to the Squaw Valley resort. I asked him how long he had been driving shuttles and he said, "About five years." I asked him if he loved his work and he said, "Oh, yes. Look at this countryside! I get to drive through it every day and share it with people from all over the world. . . . And on the weekend I get on my motorcycle and head into the wilderness with my buddies to camp out and do some fly fishing."

I asked him what he'd done before and he said he'd been a professional snowboarder, representing and demonstrating snowboards at ski resorts, until he broke his back.

"It took me a year to recover, but the doctors and therapists were so nice to me. I met friends I didn't know I had—and the resort where the accident happened picked up all my medical expenses. How blessed I was, even through that ordeal. . . ."

He asked about me and my work and finally we arrived at our destination. He bounded out of the driver's seat to help me out and acted surprised when I gave him a large tip. "Wow, I wasn't expecting this!" He laughed.

I smiled and said, "It does my heart good to see people who love what they do."

Contrast Ron's attitude with what my friend Catherine Calhoun ran into when she was running a seminar for a government agency. Catherine told me that one young man in the seminar had come up wanting to talk to her. He told her he was twenty-eight years old, had been married five years to a woman who also worked for this agency, and that he hated his job. He said, "I get a knot in my stomach starting Sunday night and I dread Monday morning when the alarm goes off. I get to work and begin counting the minutes until the day is over."

Since his wife worked in a different part of the building Catherine figured it wasn't marital strife that was causing the problem. She asked how long he'd been working there and he said, "Seven years. And I can't wait until I retire." Catherine asked if he'd ever considered doing anything else, and he replied, "Yes, but this is a very small town. I couldn't get a job anywhere that pays the salary and benefits I have here. So, I guess I'll just bite the bullet and wait for the gold watch." This young man was the same age as my shuttle driver, who probably was earning slightly above minimum wage. Who do you think was the richer of the two?

When I spoke to the same agency in another part of the country I asked the people to write down their number one goal in life. More than 90 percent of the cards came back to me with two words on them: *To Retire.*

Catherine exhorted the young clock watcher to consider doing something else—anything else—for a living. "Waiting to retire is no way to live," she said. "For my sake—for your sake—please promise me that I won't see you here when I come back next year."

"Do you think he'll do it?" I asked her.

She sighed. "I don't know. There was already a dead look in his eyes."

How sad. How tragic. How sin-full.

Show me a person who can't wait to retire and I'll show you someone who hates his or her job. I'll show you someone who has been crawling to and from work every day just waiting for the clock and the calendar to say, "You can do something else now. It's official. Now you can fly."

In a little booklet called "The Four Spiritual Laws," distributed by Campus Crusade for Christ, readers are told that "Sin means separation from God." If sin is separation from God, what could be more sin-full than choosing to devote your life energies and talents to work that does not honor God? If your work does not honor God, it does not honor you. And conversely if it does not honor you, it does not honor God.

Slavery is alive and well in America today, yet most of the chains are invisible. The keys to our freedom are always within reach—if only we stretch.

Jesus is looking at you right now, no matter how downtrodden you may be feeling. He says to you with joy—

> *Wake up, Wake up,*
> *And clothe yourself with*
> *strength.*
> *Put on your beautiful*
> *clothes.*
> *Rise from the dust,*
> *take off the slave bands*
> *from your neck . . . recognize*
> *that it is I, yes, I*
> *who speaks to you.*
>
> (Isaiah 52:1–2, 6)

Jesus looked at the people intent on killing him and said, "Destroy this temple, and in three days I will raise it up" (John 2:19). Jesus believed he could fly.

Questions

1. Is it possible to be a spiritreneur who technically works for someone else?
2. Of the two young men discussed in the chapter, who was more of a spiritreneur and why?
3. Do you believe you can fly?
4. If not, what's keeping you crawling?

Dear Lord,
I want to fly to my work in the mornings. I want my life's work to be to glorify and honor you, using my highest gifts. Help me unfold my wings from beneath my shoulder blades, and believe that I can fly.
Amen

HE GUARDED THE RIGHT
TREASURE

For where your treasure is, there will be your heart.
—Luke 12:34

Recently I met with a woman whose highest gift is painting. An award-winning designer and artist, she had put her art career on hold to raise her family. With the final child out of the home and gone, Eva now had piles of art books and supplies in every room. In fact, she had collected so much material for painting that she no longer had room in her studio to begin the process. Although several people were clamoring to commission her work, she found herself unable to begin. After a friend recommended that she get some breakthrough career counseling she called me.

We met at a local coffee shop and began to identify the obstacles that were keeping her from pursuing her spiritreneurial dream. She said, "I can't start painting until I organize my studio."

"What's keeping you from organizing your studio?"

"The feeling of being overwhelmed by the amount of stuff I've collected."

"Why not hire someone to help you?"

She replied, "Because only I can sort through what's really valuable."

"How long have you put off sorting through the material?"

"Nine months. Besides, the last time I went through the stacks of papers and files I found a check for forty-five dollars. If I just hired a stranger to throw away old papers that check might have been tossed."

There was a long silence as we sipped our tea and thought about what had been said. "Eva," I finally asked, "how many paintings are not being painted because of your clutter problem?"

"Countless," she replied.

"So the fear of tossing away a hidden forty-five-dollar check is keeping you from actualizing your lifelong dream?"

"Yes," she said, "I guess it is."

"Then you are guarding the wrong treasure."

Tears appeared in her eyes as she looked at the two pieces of paper before her. On one she had sketched her "problem"—on the other her dream of being a happy, busy, successful artist. "I guess I have been," she said. One thing that Jesus admonished us to do was to identify, and then guard, the highest treasure.

Surely few treasures could be as valuable as our God-given talents, dreams, and gifts. Yet how often do we, like the unwise entrepreneur identified in Matthew 23:13–30, bury and then guard the wrong gift? In the parable of the three talents, two spiritreneurs recognize that the treasure is not the money or talent they were given as much as it was their ability to multiply it. "Be fruitful and multiply" was the exhortation from God we received. The last was to go forth and share all that we had seen and heard the Master Multiplier do. When we guard the wrong treasures, it is those around us who ultimately suffer the loss.

Susan, a woman truck driver, had worked for years running a moving company for two owners. After they once again denied her a promotion, she got mad and quit. A single mother with two sons still at home, she took her $3,000 savings and bought her own truck. She then ran an ad in the classified section which read, "Two men and a truck will move you." She was swamped with calls. Her sons recruited their friends to help handle the demand and she kept reinvesting the profits. Three years later, she started a franchise. She is now a multi-millionaire. This woman became successful because she correctly identified the treasure she'd been given by working for years at a moving company. The treasure was not "a steady paycheck." The treasure was the knowledge, relationships, and experience God had invested in her while she was working there. Finally, she decided to take her talents and multiply them, rather than guard the paycheck she had.

I wonder how many of us are investing time and energy guarding the wrong treasures.

"A merchant goes looking for fine pearls, and when he finds one that is unusually fine, he goes and sells everything he has, and buys that pearl" (Matthew 13:45–46). When Jesus pursued his Highest gift, and left his lesser training behind, he was guarding the right treasure.

Jesus guarded the right treasure.

Questions

1. What false treasures are keeping you from multiplying your dream?
2. Identify some possible false treasures that people guard.
3. How free is a guard anyway?
4. What would friends say your hidden or unused talents are?
5. Are you willing to change your focus and let the lesser treasures go?

Dear Lord,
You are the greatest jewelry appraiser of all time. Please communicate to me in very clear ways the value you have bestowed in and on me, and then give me the courage—the sheer courage—to go out and multiply the wealth in my heart.
Amen

HE HAD IMPECCABLE MARKET TIMING

God does not lie . . . but hath in due time manifested his glory.

—Titus 1:3

One only needs to chart the timelines of Jesus' arrival in Bethlehem (at birth) and his exit from Jerusalem (at death) to realize that his entry into the marketplace was perfectly timed to maximize God's prophets. He was born, for example, in year zero and died A.D. 33. This assumes you are using the standard American calendar for measurement, and not the Jewish calendar or the Chinese calendar or the Aztec calendar. One would think that Jesus was known for his split-second timing regarding financial decisions, strategic meetings, and being at the wheel of the ship when the storms came.

Actually, Scripture reveals that Jesus was late paying his taxes; was late getting to Lazarus, and was asleep in the boat when conceivably he should have been on deck, on the alert when a major storm came (Matthew 17:27; John 11:5–22; Luke 8:23).

As I study and meet successful spiritreneurs, I am struck by their impeccable market timing. Susanna Palomares and Dave Cowan, for example, were able to perfectly time the sale of their California home—skillfully navigating the highs and lows of the resale market to reap the benefits of the upsurge in the market. When I asked them how they were able to figure out when to sell, Dave smiled and said, "We agreed that we would sell the place only after Susanna's horse died. When 'Paloosa' died, we sold."

There is so much talk these days about "market timing" and "windows of opportunity" that the underlying message is, "Success only comes around once, and you'd better grab it while you can." Yet any reading of business literature shows companies that are "built to last" are not so concerned with split-second transactions as they are with the warm and long-lasting handshakes of happy customers, and the smile that spreads slowly across a satisfied customer's face.

Granted, technology has changed the pace with which we make decisions. Everything is so speeded up now that our spirits rarely have time to catch up with our bodies. Gone are the days when we had time to sit on the front porch and visit with the neighbors. This morning, for example, I arose at 5:00 A.M. to feed the horses on my Texas ranch. Starbucks, my weanling colt, had cut his jaw on a fence the day before, so I administered antibiotics through a syringe as the dogs barked around my feet. At 5:00 P.M. I was sitting in a restaurant atop a skyscraper in Manhattan, wearing my best business suit as two people discussed new opportunities with me. Tonight, as I lie on my heavenly bed in a Westin Hotel and write this, I can't help but wonder if the human soul and psyche were meant to live and move at this pace—from one reality to another. Add to that pace the undercurrent of fear that one is going to miss the perfect timing to buy or sell, launch or merge, downsize or upgrade or add value, and you've got a lot of pressure on a body.

If you are a spiritreneur, your work is eternal. So, although it may seem that your timing might be less than perfect when viewed against all the measurables, you can take heart knowing that in God there is no time. And in God there is all time. Therefore, how can you be late?

I read about a woman who noticed that the wipes she used on her baby's bottom were always cold. She then created a device that warmed wipes, and with her and her husband's savings launched a company called Warm Wipes. Following the conventional wisdom that licensing the product to a larger entity would be a way to create passive income, she found herself wined and dined by a fairly well-known distributor of baby products. I can imagine she and her husband celebrating the timing of their deal, striking while the iron was hot.

However, this distributor did nothing with the Warm Wipes but sit on them, so to speak, until his company was wiped out in bankruptcy. Forbidden by her contract to make or sell competing products for three years, "Wanda" found herself fretting as other companies developed competing products. By the time the corpse of her distributor's company was buried, Wanda had lost her lead in the "warm wipe" industry. But she did not let her first mistake in timing deter her. Waiting for the bankruptcy dust to settle, Wanda and her husband created several other innovative products and formed a new company called Baby Comforts, which incorporated a full line of products that made babies more comfortable as they went about their daily tasks of growing, rolling over, and taking their first steps.

So, was Wanda's poorly timed contract with the doomed distributor a failure, or an ultimate success?

A young Walt Disney lost the rights to Oswald the Rabbit, his first beloved cartoon drawing, when another company bought the rights from his employer. In the train on the way home from that defeat, Walt sketched a mouse with two big ears, a big smile, and huge potential, and decided to go out on his own. Was the timing of the loss of Oswald the Rabbit a failure for Disney, or a success?

Ultimately, if we dance only to the hands of a watch or the dates in a calendar, we are pursuing a limited goal. Are we to be wise in the timing of our decisions? Absolutely. Are we to obsess about them? Absolutely not. For our God is an awesome God—one whose specialty is Just in Time Delivery—no matter what the dates may look like on your calendar.

"Trust in the Lord, and do good; dwell in the land and enjoy safe pasture. Be still before the Lord and wait patiently for him. . . . Commit your way to the Lord; trust in him and he will do this" (Psalms 37:4–7).

Jesus had impeccable market timing.

Questions

1. Are you obsessive about the timing of your actions?
2. What amount of energy is tied up by trying to calculate exactly when to get in or out, or when to begin?
3. What other stories about "being in a hurry" and missing God's timing come to mind?

Dear Lord,
Help me to realize that in you, my work is eternal. Help me
tune in not so much to the rise and fall of markets, but to
the rising and falling of your breathing as you lie here be-
side me—my King, my Lover, my Life, my all.

                                                Amen

HE WAS WILLING TO WALK AWAY

*But Jesus said, "Follow me and leave the dead to
bury the dead."*

—Matthew 8:21

One principle in negotiating is that the person who is willing
to walk away from the table is the one who holds the most
power. This, in fact, is a spiritual principle that has nothing to
do with lack of commitment but everything to do with nonat-
tachment—to anything that would become a "god" to you.

Jesus had to walk away from his father's carpenter shop in
order to fulfill his mission. Being willing to walk away is a key
characteristic of spiritreneurs. We had to be willing to walk
away from the security of what we knew to enter the unknown,
and we must be willing to walk away from what we create if it
starts running us and not vice versa.

Recently I spent a glorious weekend in the Adirondack
Mountains with my friends Dave Cowan and Susanna
Palomares. In the space of 48 hours I met three spiritreneurs
I will remember for the rest of my life.

Brother Gregory is a monk at the Skete monastery in New York. I met him when we were walking alongside the kennels. Every monastery has to be self-supporting and the Skete Monastery is famous for its German shepherd puppies. There is a three-year waiting list for these incredible dogs, and Susanna wanted us to drive up to make an application for one. As we walked up a glorious, golden, tree-lined hill, we were met at the top by Brother Gregory. A rosy-cheeked man with a robust laugh, he offered to take us inside the kennels to play with the puppies. As we talked I asked him how he came to be assigned to the kennels. He said that he had grown up in New York City, and one day his father brought home a German shepherd. However, they soon had to move to a place where dogs were not allowed. He got tears in his eyes as he remembered having to give away his beautiful German shepherd. He said, "I remember feeling that I could be happy the rest of my life if only I could be around these beautiful dogs."

After several unsatisfying stints working in corporate America, he decided to become a Russian Orthodox monk. "I applied to the monastery and lo and behold they placed me here—as the man in charge of their world-famous German shepherd kennels." He threw his head back and laughed as a black ball of puppy fur squirmed in his arms trying to lick his face, the sun streaming in through the maple trees behind them.

"Now there is a happy man," I said to myself. He walked away from the world and God led him straight to his bliss. Brother Gregory is a spiritreneur—because he walked away.

Later that day Dave and Susanna took me to meet Ralph Kylloe.

"Is he there?" Dave questioned as we approached. "Yes he is. The flag is up!" said Susanna as we stopped the car and got out and entered another world in another time. Ralph Kylloe is a collector and distributor of rustic, authentic, handmade Adirondack furniture. As Dave, Susanna, and Ralph exchanged greetings I was drawn to a chair made of handrubbed beryl wood, supported on legs made of huge naturally shed moose antlers. On the counter were several copies of magazines like *Country Living* and *Home and Garden* that featured Ralph's work. His wife, Michelle, was behind the counter, taking an order over the phone, and Ralph was holding their eight-month-old daughter, Lindsey, in his arms. She looked like a forest nymph with big blue eyes and a toothless smile. I asked Ralph how he got started and he said, "I was a student at Harvard and one day my college roommate brought home a rustic piece of furniture he'd picked up at a flea market up here. I took one look at that chair and said, 'That's it, I just found my calling.' I left all my Harvard buddies to come here to start collecting and I've never looked back. Now they sell stocks and I sell sticks." He laughed. "But I wouldn't trade my life for theirs for anything."

"There's a happy man," I said as we drove away. Ralph Kylloe walked away from a future working in skyscrapers and became rich in the forest instead—designing and distributing "bliss on a stick."

The other spiritreneur I met with that weekend was Susanna. Once an owner of a publishing company that specialized in distributing training materials to schools and counselors, she turned over ownership to an associate so she could walk away from the administrative duties and chores that running a business entails. Now she's free to write the books she used to have to write *and* sell.

"The check I get from the company is smaller now," she admitted. "But the peace I have is immeasurable."

"See the license plate on the car in front of us?" Dave pointed as we were driving. "It's the New Hampshire state motto."

I looked closer and read, "Live Free or Die."

"That's a great motto to live by, isn't it?" Dave laughed.

Live free or die.

Jesus was willing to walk away.

Questions

1. Is your motto "Live Free or Die"? If not, what is it?
2. What is holding you back from pursuing your bliss?
3. Do you feel it is possible to really earn a living—make a life—doing what you love?
4. What were the risks that Jesus took in walking away from the carpenter shop? What were his rewards?
5. What will be yours?

Dear Lord,
Let me trust you like Ralph and Susanna and Dave and a puppy-loving monk named Gregory. Let me trust you to lead me to my bliss.
Amen

HE SAID, "YOU CAN"

For with God, all things are possible.
—Matthew 10:27

I recently did some career counseling with a human resource director who was three years away from retiring. She wanted to start her own business and was wisely preparing in advance. A self-confirmed workaholic, she was planning either to start an interior decorating/home remodeling service or purchase a day spa. After listening to her schedule for the last three years (which included dealing with a divorce, the death of her mother, and an extremely hostile work environment), I realized that the last thing she needed to do was take on the headache of owning and running a health spa. I told her, "I suspect what you're secretly yearning for is some guilt-free time as a guest at a spa." I paused, and then added, "You know, you don't have to own one to spend time there."

There was a long silence, and then she burst out laughing. "You're right!" she exclaimed. "I have never given myself the luxury of a full day at a spa."

"Well, as your 'career doctor,' " I said, laughing with her, "I hereby prescribe that you get two massages and one facial, manicure, and pedicure per month. You need it, you deserve it, and I guarantee it will cost a lot less and reward you far more than owning your own spa."

When she began to explain why she couldn't afford the time for two massages and a spa treatment, I listened for a while and then said, "Don't tell me why you can't do it—tell me why you can."

I met a man not too long ago who was saying that his most recent discovery about himself was that he loved to dance. He had gone to his granddaughter's high school graduation ball and found himself moving around the dance floor like a twenty-year-old. When I asked him if he could take ballroom dancing lessons in his hometown in California, he began to share a long list of reasons why he couldn't, such as "You have to have a partner . . . I'm not sure I could make the Saturday classes . . . I'm not really competitive," etc. Finally, I looked him square in the face and said, "Jim, don't tell me why you can't—tell me why you can!"

In my Path training seminars, which are designed to help people find their life mission, we do an exercise that calls for people to write down a long list of obstacles and fears that are preventing them from fulfilling their dreams. Then they trade lists with the person sitting next to them, who proceeds to help eliminate each obstacle or fear by replacing it with an obvious opportunity or strength. The benefit people get out of this exercise is seeing how minor other people's obstacles seem to be, compared to their own. What seems like a huge hurdle to you can be seen as a mere stepping-stone in the eyes of your more objective neighbor. So I say to people at the end of this process:

"Now—don't tell me why you can't,
tell me why you can."

When an idea hits you—whether it's a new business of your own or something different you want to try at work, it seems like the doors of heaven are swinging open for you, yet almost immediately the little bricks of "I can't" begin to start piling up, one by one, blocking your dreams. (Quite often friends, family, bosses, coworkers come by and drop off a brick or two.) The fastest way to overcome these excuses is to begin to write out on paper every possible reason why you *can* do what you are dreaming.

Jesus looked at the man paralyzed in fear. "Get up and walk," Jesus said, reaching out his hand (Matthew 9:1–8).

Jesus said, "You can."

Questions

1. Make a list of all the reasons you can't do what you're dreaming of.
2. Hand this list to someone who wants only the best for you, and have them obliterate each of your obstacles/excuses.
3. Now, make a list of all the reasons you can live your dream, including as many scriptural references as you can.

Dear Lord,
Nothing is impossible to you or through you. Help me sur-
round myself with people who believe in me, and hear
their affirmations of my abilities and opportunities in you.
Amen

HE DEFINED HIS SUCCESS BEFORE HE BEGAN

I seek the will of my Father.
—John 5:30

The more I work with business leaders, the more I become convinced that we are each striving for one thing with all our heart and soul and mind and strength—to live our personal definition of success. All our activities and behaviors stem from and return to that core word and value: *Success.* Some people might say that Jesus had no desire to be successful. They would be wrong.

Jesus wanted more than anything to be successful. He said it was what drove him, what haunted him. He had such a yearning for it that he was willing to give up everything to get it. Jesus' definition of success was "to do the will of God." He said it was his food, his delight, his pleasure, and his reason for being. He sought it from his childhood, and kept it as his compass, his light, his ladder, his altar, and his final prayer.

Jesus defined his success before he began. If we are not clear about what true success looks like, how will we know when we get there?

William was tall, handsome, and confident. A successful consultant for one of the leading business firms in Europe, he was being invited to step into a partnership role—one that would place him among his company's elite. He'd also received an offer to teach at a university in his hometown. He had just returned form leading a large consulting project in Africa, and was set to return there the following week. As we talked I could tell that he was torn about his firm's offer. At dinner that night, he sat next to me and I asked him about his life. His wife was divorcing him. Married only five years, with a four-year-old son, they were separating over several issues—William's infidelity being one of them. He had openly cheated on her while she was pregnant.

His wife, Sarah, was also a successful consultant. Their demanding travel schedules didn't make maintaining a home life an easy task. Maybe it was the dim light—maybe it was the schnapps—but soon William revealed to me that his father had never married his mother. He had sired three children in one marriage, fathered William, returned to his first marriage to father more children, then left that wife to marry yet another woman and have two more children. William was the only one who never knew his father, nor received his legitimate name. "He was a world-class athlete, though," he said, his eyes brightening a bit. "I know that much about him."

Suddenly the family pattern became clear. "So, William," I asked gently, "what does success really look like to you?

Repeating your father's womanizing ways and abandoning your son?" Tears began to roll down his cheeks as he gasped in pain at the truth of my words. I paused for a moment before I continued. "Your choice now, is it to be a world-class, globe-trotting, high-vaulting consultant? Or could you really consider this teaching job?" He looked at me with tear-filled eyes, pleading with me to both stop and continue. "What does success really look like? Not to the world—but to you?"

He struggled to catch his breath and then said in a whisper, "To be a good husband and father." He put his head down on the table and wept out loud as the waves of pain and hurt swept over him.

Waiting for a few moments for his grief to subside, I quietly continued prodding. "Give me a vision of what a good husband and father looks like."

"I don't know," he said.

"Just try," I urged.

"Well, I'm home every day to pick him up from school. I can see myself carrying him on my shoulders as we walk through a field. My wife is carrying our new little girl . . ." Again he started sobbing. "Our family is together. My wife knows that I adore her. Together we're building a happy home."

There was a long silence. "I know what I have to do," he said. "I have a lot of fences to mend."

I smiled. "With God's help you can. But, it's going to take hard work."

"Harder than running a consulting project in Asia?" he asked.

"Way harder than that."

Maybe I will never see William again. Maybe William will try teaching. If he does, I know that he'll have some hard-won lessons to impart. Whatever he chooses, William's choice will be determined by his definition of success.

And so it is with you and me.

At every opportunity—we must ask ourselves, What is success?

Your life reveals your choices.

Jesus defined success before he began.

Questions

1. Write down your personal definition of success.
2. How would your definition of success compare with Jesus'?
3. Is your life out of balance?
4. Could it be that you are working toward an inadequate definition of success, one that isn't large enough to fill your soul?

Dear Lord,
Help me be very clear about my definition of success. And most of all, may it match yours.
                                                    Amen

HE DIDN'T WORK FOR MONEY

*Do not work for food that spoils, but for food which
endures to eternal life.*

—John 6:27

The World Business Academy is an international network of
business executives and entrepreneurs who use their skills
and resources in the creation of a positive future for the planet.
In a recent issue of their quarterly journal I was delighted to
read the following comments by Claude Morgan Lewenz, an
American businessman living in New Zealand. The editor had
asked Claude to send an author's bio for an article he had written in an earlier issue. Claude said, "If I tried to explain in cog-
nitive, definitive words what I am doing . . . the words would be
like the dried trail of a snail." His résumé would include titles
such as entrepreneur, founder of computer software companies,
a changer of the concept of local government, a builder of post-
graduate schools of classical studies, village designer, builder
of environmentally sustainable housing prototypes, patron of
the arts, and a retiree at the age of forty-seven. When asked how

he made so much money, he replied, "My trend has been to select an area where the energy is interesting, to immerse myself in it, and then make five years' income in a week—but never know in advance that this will happen.

"What I am is a person who does not work for a living, who has no inheritance to look to, who channels immense amounts of energy in a coherent way, and who is always surprised when he finds that financially he is rather comfortable. Yes, I work hard, but I don't work for money. It just happens to be a by-product of my focus. Several times I have had a bit of a shock when I would find that we were quite out of money, flat broke, checks a-bouncing, and I would have to scrounge wood to heat our home [in the middle of winter on a Rhode Island coastal island]. Then, pleasantly, a record-setting contract would float in, and suddenly our accountant was saying we had a tax problem and had to buy a West Coast software company ten times as big as ours or face huge tax bills."

I was delighted with Claude for putting into words one of the key requirements of being a spiritreneur. Spiritreneurs do not work for money. Instead, we channel tremendous amounts of energy into areas that interest us, and find, surprisingly, that money is a by-product of our loving and intense focus.

I saw a bumper sticker recently that read "I thought I wanted a career. But I found out that all I really wanted was a paycheck." However, according to the Sloan Management Review, money is not the number one goal of today's workers. In a recent article, Ian Mitroff and Elizabeth Denton showed that interviewees rank the elements of their jobs that give them meaning and purpose as follows:

1. The ability to realize their full potential
2. Being associated with an organization that is good and ethical
3. Interesting work
4. Making money
5. Having good colleagues; serving humankind
6. Service to future generations
7. Service to their immediate communities

Jesus told us repeatedly that if we seek first the kingdom of God, all else will be added unto us.

Meaning truly is more important than money. A recent article in the *Trend* newsletter stated that many of today's sudden millionaires are finding themselves at odds—with their neighbors, their children, their spouses, and even themselves. Proverbs 13:11 states, "Wealth gotten by vanity quickly disappears." The luxury of having nothing to do quite often leads to misery. We need to work in order to find meaning, and spiritreneurs have found their meaningful work on earth.

What joy, what bliss we experience when we align our will, our work, and our talents with those of our Creator. We can then be like the stress-free lilies of the field, clothed in raiment more beautiful than Solomon's. Jesus said, "My food is to do the will of the One who sent me."

Jesus did not work for money.

Questions

1. Would you continue to do what you do if you never received a dime for it?
2. What do you work for?
3. List the reasons you work.

Dear Lord,
Teach me to hunger for your food, and not for things that
do not feed the soul.
                    Amen

HE WAS AN INSIDER

And the Word became flesh, and dwelt among us.
—John 1:14

B ecause Jesus is so renowned, it is easy to forget that at one time he did not stand out at all. He easily blended into the crowd. Even though he came from heaven, God saw fit to make him fit into this world—as part of a village, part of a race, part of a region, part of a culture. Jesus of Nazareth. Jewish male. Average height and build. Son of Mary and Joseph. Occupation: carpenter. Address: Olive Avenue.

Thus in some ways Jesus was an insider—part of a larger system of people and customs, tastes, and times. Jesus totally blended in, until he didn't.

Perhaps because you work in a large organization and feel no inclination to launch into a solo enterprise, you feel you cannot be a spiritreneur. That is not so. You can still dramatically affect the flavor of the stew that is your community.

In fact, employees have driven the resurgence of interest in spirituality in large business organizations across the country. *Business Week* magazine had a cover story about the phenomenon of employees challenging their bosses to allow and integrate spiritual discussions in the workplace.

Many employees have launched study groups that meet during the lunch hour for book reviews and discussions, or to learn more about their faiths. I have been delighted at the diversity of the groups that have called our offices, letting us know that they are studying *Jesus, CEO* at major pharmaceutical firms and banks, and there's even one group called "The Cigar-Smoking, Foot-Stomping Sons of Guns" that called us from Chicago.

We heard recently from a border patrol agent who was being reprimanded for insisting that some undocumented aliens be fed before they were sent back across the border. He said, "They had been traveling in the desert for days. There were women and children among them. They were so hungry and so thirsty that I couldn't just put them on the bus and send them away without seeing to their needs." He had been reading my book and it gave him the courage, he said, to act on his conscience. He purchased several more copies to send upstream to his superiors. This is one "insider" acting like a spiritreneur, integrating his beliefs into his work.

Richard Barrett, vice president of the World Bank, started a small study group with his friends to discuss spiritual issues in the workplace. The small handful soon grew to four hundred people—all meeting on their own time, all employees of the bank, all wanting to know more about how to make a difference in the world. A financial institution seems like an unlikely place for people to be seeking larger meaning, doesn't it? But then again, where better? Spiritual issues and needs run deep in every human heart, no matter what uniforms they wear or calculators they may carry in their cases.

Search for meaning can begin anywhere, at any time. All that is required is for one person to say, "Would you like to meet and discuss spiritual issues—with an open mind?"

St. Vincent's Hospital in Indianapolis now has a Spiritual Retreat Center called Seton Cove, built specifically for the needs of its employees on a lovely few acres situated by a pond. Sister Sharon Richardt, the brains behind the center, said, "We studied all major religions, and determined that the four things each had in common for retreats were: study, meditation, reflection, and direction. We have integrated these components so that employees from different faith backgrounds can come here and be renewed." Sister Sharon is a spiritreneur—an insider working within a larger system, to make a difference.

Salt is almost infinitesimally small, yet each granule can pack a powerful wallop. Salt is a preservative against rot and decay. Salt acts as a preventative, helping the body fend off disease. Salt is curative, helping tissues and muscles mend.

Roman soldiers used to be paid not with gold coins but with salt. Hence the saying, "He is worth his salt." It's where the word *salary* came from.

Are you worth your salt, your salary?

This morning my newborn filly, Little Pistol, discovered the salt lick in the pasture. She is in her oral phase, tasting and licking everything, and sometimes it's good, sometimes it's not so good. This morning I watched as she nudged over to the block and started licking, slowly at first. Her little tail began wagging in excitement and she began to stomp her feet. This was a new flavor, out there in the middle of the open field. What she had discovered was a very good thing.

What kind of salt lick are you? Still salty, or so run-down that you are only fit for being trampled underfoot?

Jesus said, "Ye are the salt of the earth. But if the salt has lost its savor, what good is it?" (Luke 14:34).

Jesus was an insider.

Questions

1. Do you feel that you are too small or insignificant to make a difference in your corporate culture?
2. Have you ever tasted a stew that didn't have enough salt?
3. Is your organization like that?
4. What would it look like if you became a little saltier in your workplace? In your community?

Dear Lord,
I feel like an insider, but too small to make much of a dif-
ference. Help me see the significance of what a few grains
of salt can do.
        Amen

HE SURRENDERED

Into your hands I commit my spirit.
                                                    —Luke 23:46

Two years ago I was invited to co-lead a Journey in Faith tour to the Holy Land. The tour was designed to inspire leadership skills by having people walk in the footsteps of Christ. Not knowing what to expect, but trusting the friend who sent me, I showed up and stepped backward in time with a handful of other pilgrims.

I had cleverly gathered up the tools I had, my field guides and books, *Jesus, CEO* and *The Path,* thinking these would come in handy. Yet as the tour progressed I found that I was able to say less, rather than more. Scott Shearer, the tour leader, aptly said, "A pilgrimage is a journey to a place that takes you deeper inside your soul."

The Holy Land is not like any place I had ever been. Unlike tours of Europe or the famous cities in the United States, the popular sites had nothing to do with battles won or celebrities spotted. Every celebrity-inspired or pride-of-victory historical site I had ever seen paled in significance to these holy, dusty places where Jesus walked.

I learned that Jesus was not placed in a manger, but a stone feeding trough. He wasn't born in a stable, but a cave. In fact, the homes of those days were often carved out of caves. Jesus and his friends often slept in the caves outside of Jerusalem. The prison in which he was kept was actually a limestone cave, carved out underneath the grounds of Caiphas palace. The rock where Jesus stood and took a little boy's loaves and fishes, blessing and multiplying them to feed a crowd of five thousand, is a rock barely two feet long and maybe three feet wide.

As we walked to each site—the Sea of Galilee, the garden of Gethsemane—I began to realize that these incredible holy sites had nothing to do with victory and everything to do with surrender.

Here is where Mary surrendered to the will of God, and said yes to the birth of Jesus. Here is where Peter dropped his nets, and surrendered his life to the man on the shore. Here is where the little boy surrendered his lunch so the crowd could be fed. Here is where Jesus surrendered to the guards who had come looking for him. Here is where he surrendered his life.

I am still, to this day, trying to absorb the meaning of what we saw there. How antithetical it is to teach and preach surrender.

When I got home, I joked with Mike Regan, the friend who sent me, "Hey, I'm from Texas. We are raised to shout 'Remember the Alamo! We will never surrender!' "

In a recent interview in *Fast Company* magazine, iconoclast computer visionary Avram Miller said, "Today, when Intel builds a new factory, it is investing $2 billion in product it hasn't designed for markets that don't exist. This is hard for American businessmen, and I say 'men' because in order to do this, you have to give up control, and giving up control makes guys really miserable. Control is an illusion. I don't think it ever existed, but now even the illusion is gone."

How different and how simple, really, is the path to glory. Recognize that you are not in control. And then let God do the rest.

At the National Prayer Breakfast I ran into a business leader friend of mine. He had earlier resigned as president of his publicly traded company, only to be brought back by a special request from the board. As we shared a few precious moments together, he asked me about my trip to the Holy Land. I told him what I had learned—that the only path to glory lies in surrender. He stopped eating his sandwich and put his head down for a moment. "I needed to hear that today," he said. "I was just about to go into the board meeting and tell them we have to go for the jugular veins of our competition." He smiled at the irony. "How much we have yet to learn," he said and patted my hand.

How do we integrate surrender into the business plan? I struggle with the question daily. Yet I am convinced that only in surrender can we ever taste victory.

This is the irony of the spiritreneur. We will get where we need to be only by admitting we do not know the way.

"Into your hands I commit my spirit," Jesus said.
Jesus surrendered.

Questions

1. How does the concept of surrender strike you as a leadership tool?
2. Where in your endeavor or enterprise do you need to surrender?
3. What does surrender mean to you?
4. What could be the possible outcomes?
5. Who are you surrendering to? how? when? and why?

Dear Lord,
Here I am trying to be a conqueror, when all I need do to attain victory in you is surrender. Take my ignorance and my vulnerability and fear and let your power and glory shine through. I give you my sword, in order that I might wear your robe.
Amen

HE SAID, "BELIEVE IT—OR NOT"

Be not afraid—only believe.
—Mark 5:36

M y four-year-old godson, Jacob, has a new favorite phrase. Lately, he begins every sentence with "Believe it or not." "Laurie, believe it or not, when you catch a lizard by its tail, it will leave its tail wiggling in your hands and get away. And then," he added with a gasp, "it will grow another one!" He looked at me with widened eyes to see if I caught the wonder of it. Believe it, or not.

At a birthday party I attended yesterday seven-year-old Clarissa brought out a book she wanted to read to me. It was the story of Charles Ripley's *Believe It or Not!*

As her seven-year-old reading skills slipped, sped, and sometimes tumbled over the words in the book, I was fascinated to learn more about a man who decided that the world was full of wonder. He set out to explore—and prove it. There were photographs of him standing next to the wasp-waisted man in New Guinea, a man with four pupils in his eyes from China, and a two-headed kitten playing with a ball of yarn. In another photo he was conversing with a plate-lipped woman from the Ubangi tribe. Another photo showed him sitting atop a donkey in front of the pyramids, continuing his search for the unusual and real.

The book showed pictures of him being mobbed by fans— all seeking his signature on a piece of paper. The caption read, "Ripley receives more autograph requests than the President!" How the crowd rushes toward those who show us that there's more to the world than we think—who inspire us with wonder and awe.

Jesus was such a man, saying, "The blind will see . . . the deaf will hear . . . the lame will dance for joy." He turned water into wine and said, "Believe it—or not."

He raised Lazarus from the dead and said, "Believe it—or not." He fed five thousand people with five loaves and said, "Believe it—or not, when you share what you have, more will be given to you. When you are the very lowest in your spirit, is when you'll see God. When you give a cup of water even to a beggar on the street, you have done so to me. I love you dearly—believe it—or not."

What we believe determines our actions. Our actions determine our future. Jesus stood there—stands there before us— offering us the very power of God, and says, "Believe it—and you'll soar. The choice is up to you."

Do you believe the vision you've been given? As spiritreneurs we are daily confronted with circumstances that don't seem to be going our way.

When a bank turns us down for a loan, do we accept their lack of belief in us—or keep searching until we find a resonating partner? When the forty-ninth call we've made that day is still No, do we accept defeat as our fate, or do we keep calling until we find the Yes that has been hidden like an Easter egg deep in the bushes.

A friend of mine was sharing that she had been disillusioned after meeting some of the leaders in the spirituality movement. "Some of them are so phony," she complained. I thought a moment and then said, "When we are disillusioned it means we never had a belief in the first place—only an illusion."

Believe—and you will be healed.

Believe—and you will be saved.

Believe—and you will experience victory.

That is what Jesus says.

When *Jesus, CEO* was first presented to publishers, at least seven of them turned it down. With each rejection notice, believe it or not, I got more excited. I knew that statistically, the more No's I got meant I was getting closer to the Yes I needed.

Because when God gives you a vision, you either believe it, or you don't.

Jesus said, "Believe it—or not."

Questions

1. Do you really believe the vision you've been given?
2. What will the consequences be if you don't?
3. What could the outcomes be if you do?

Dear Lord,
You've demonstrated time and again that we live in a universe with wonders beyond measure, love beyond fathoming, abundance beyond our wildest imaginings. Help me to believe—and leave the No's behind me.

Amen

HE KNEW YOU CAN'T FIX WHAT ISN'T BROKEN

He has sent me to bind up the broken-hearted.
—Isaiah 61:11

Spiritreneurs have an eye for broken things. Maybe it's as simple as a broken connection between customers and suppliers. A spiritreneur might see that customers are not being served, and step in to fill in the gap.

Spiritreneurs are highly attuned to two things. The first is the voice within that says, "I can do this better than I am doing it," and the second is the voice that says, "I can do this better than they are doing it." The frustration of spiritreneurs is not a lack of opportunity, it is that there is not enough time—not enough people—to do what needs to be done.

Jesus displayed this spirit when he exhorted his disciples to "Pray for more workers because the harvest is ripe" (Luke 10:2).

While attending the University of California at Santa Barbara, Paul Orfalea got irritated at constantly having to wait in line to get copies made for his classes. To add insult to injury, he and his classmates were paying exorbitant prices for each of the copies they got. He decided to fix it. He bought his own copier, rented a former hamburger stand across the street from his competitor, and started selling copies at half the price. Thus was Kinko's born—a multimillion-dollar operation that now caters to small business owners as well as students. Orfalea saw a problem and decided to fix it.

Bobbi Brown was a homemaker who didn't like the unnatural shades of lipstick and nail poish she found in the stores. So, she brewed up her own batch of more natural colors, and began selling them to her friends. Now Bobbi Brown is a brand, not just a dissatisfied consumer—simply because she saw something that wasn't working and decided to fix it.

Enterprising landscapers in a San Diego neighborhood drop off little plastic bags full of gravel into the yards of people who obviously don't have time to mow or tend their yard. (I used to make it my goal that my lawn would be so well tended that I would never get one of their little gravel bags.) "No time to mow the lawn? Let us do it for you! Tired of having a lawn? We can install desert landscaping!" The company deposits their little promo bags only in the yards of people who obviously have a problem that needs to be solved. This is the entrepreneurial spirit—look for something that's broken and fix it. And the truth is, we live in a broken world. Opportunities for service and for improving the human condition abound.

After I had given a lecture on *Jesus, CEO* to a group of university students I was stunned when a young man approached me and said, "Why don't you write a book that says what we all know here—that everything has already been done. There's nothing left for our generation to do!" My first instinct was to climb off the podium and engage him until his eyes—which were obviously closed—popped open in a sudden awareness of a) the value of life, particularly his own, and b) the desire to live just for the privilege of taking one more breath. But I simply stared at him, dumbfounded.

"Already been done!" I exclaimed. "What's already been done? Can't you see the suffering in the world today? Barring that, don't you know that the human spirit is limitless in God to create—to invent, to improve? If it's already been done, then why are you and I standing here talking instead of playing our harps on cloud nine?"

Seldom have I felt so angry at a question or comment. The very thought that there's nothing left to do runs counter to every cell in a spiritreneur's body. At night our very muscles twitch in anticipation of work we could be doing. I wonder about that boy's future. Where does such blind despair come from? Watching too much TV perhaps? Or listening to the news?

I feel that every person has the ability to be a spiritreneur. Maybe I'm wrong. Maybe most people want to file into lines that have been drawn for them, and sit in boxes that all look alike, and collect a paycheck like clockwork so they can go home and pick up a remote that turns on a box that numbs their brain. My friend Arnie says it's true. That for all the motivational books people read and all the seminars they attend, fewer than one in a hundred will make a change as a result of new information.

I thought about it a minute and said, "Well, it's the one in a hundred we must go for."

If it ain't broke, you can't fix it. Jesus said if your soul isn't dirty, then I can't help you. If you know it all, have it all, have done it all, and feel not even an inch of something lacking, then I can have no part of you. But, oh, if you realize the huge gaps in your soul—between who you are and who you want to be—then you and I can be partners. Your gaps will be my strength. Your arms will be my arms. And together, we can change things—make them better than they are.

"If I do not wash you, you can have no share with me" (John 13:8).

Jesus knew you can't fix what isn't broken.

Questions

1. What opportunity(ies) do you see as a result of broken things/relationships/systems around you? List five.
2. What qualifies you to fix it?
3. What would the "fixed" thing look like?

Dear Lord,
The very essence of your nature is fixing broken things—broken hearts, broken lives, broken lines of communication. Give me your vision to see all things being whole. Let me use my gifts and talents to help fix a broken world.
Amen

HE SAW THROUGH A LARGER
WINDOW

Open your eyes, and look at the fields!
—John 4:35

When Jesus was working in his father's carpenter shop I imagine that he often looked out the window. Even as he was busy fashioning tables or chairs I'm sure he couldn't help but notice situations in the village that were not right. The way the prostitutes were scorned and spit upon . . . the way the lepers were treated . . . the way money was changing hands outside the temple. Spiritreneurs see the world through a larger window, just as he did.

The founder of the Grameen Bank, Muhammed Yunus, was originally an economics professor, earning a comfortable living teaching theory to the brightest students. But as he was teaching economics in Bangladesh his countrymen were dying of starvation on the city streets. He began to do research into the true needs of the poor and was ashamed and astonished to learn that some people in his village were trapped in a system of poverty because of the lack of twenty-seven dollars. Not twenty-seven dollars to buy food, but twenty-seven dollars to buy raw materials to make bamboo stools. He dug a little deeper and realized that with a loan of twenty-seven dollars he could lift 122 families in the village out of the grip of usurious local loan sharks.

He put up the $27 himself, then offered to personally guarantee up to $300 in microloans to the poorest of the poor. What began as a glance outside his window became the foundation for the now internationally recognized and duplicated Grameen Bank. Muhammed, a compassionate Muslim, became a spiritreneur, using his training in economics to lift millions out of poverty. The Grameen Bank now loans out more than $250 million in microloans a year, almost exclusively to impoverished women. And does the money come back? Yes! These women have a payback rate of 95 percent! Muhammed looked out a larger window, and his heart caught fire.

Deborah Bartlett is also a spiritreneur. Trained as a reporter and talk show host in Chicago, she returned to her homeland in the Bahamas and began to use her training and influence to uplift the working conditions—and mental framework—of her fellow Bahamians. She organized the first international conference of CEOs, bringing in some of the world's leading entrepreneurs to teach and challenge the locals to rise to a new level of ethics and excellence.

Deborah enlisted business leaders to provide scholarships to promising students. She insisted that politicians as well as high school students be able to state their personal mission statement in a single sentence. She personally financed the

CEO conference and trained volunteers, creating an annual event that brings millions of dollars and networking opportunities to those in her country. She arranged for me to lead the entire assembled Parliament of the British Virgin Islands in developing a mission statement in a half-day workshop. "Politicians must be especially clear about what they came here to do," she said, with fire in her eyes.

Deborah could simply just have created wealth for herself. But she looks out a larger window, and sees the entire Caribbean as her personal responsibility to challenge, support, and inspire. I call her "The Joan of Arc of the Caribbean." She is as happy talking to the dishwashers in the kitchen as she is interviewing kings and prime ministers. The saying in the Bahamas is "You can't say no to Debbie." The truth is, no one wants to, because she is truly an anointed spiritreneur—looking out a larger window—with the lives of so many in mind.

An economics professor. A television reporter. Each changing history because of their "unique view" of the world.

Jesus looked out a larger window.

Questions

1. What do you see out your window every day?
2. What would you see if your window were somehow enlarged?
3. Describe the view as you think Jesus might see it.
4. What training or talents could you engage to make that view a more beautiful one? One more just and fair?
5. What now will you do?

Dear Lord,

Enlarge my window and my heart—to see and feel what you do, when you look upon my world. Set my heart on fire so much that my mind is illuminated and refined, my soul is purified, as I set my hands to work—being your hands in the world.

Amen

HE SAID, "I SEE YOU"

He hath opened my eyes.
—John 9:30

The success of any spiritreneur will ultimately depend on whether or not these three words are true: *I see you.* To see someone—truly *see* them—is to honor and respect them. Not for what they can bring to you, but simply because they are. It is when people don't feel seen or heard that they begin to boil. Unseen customers disappear. Unseen coworkers resign. Unseen family members will burn down your fields, if that's what it takes to be seen.

King David was a very busy man. When he wasn't out killing Philistines, he was writing songs and ruling over Israel. He was—in every material term of the word—a full-blown success. But even he had problems with his kids, one of them in particular. Absalom was his most beautiful son and also his most quick-tempered. When Absalom, in a fury, killed one of David's top men, he was banished from the palace. David did not want to speak to him again.

Absalom, craving his father's forgiveness, sent messenger after messenger to King David. All were ignored. Finally, in a desperate bid to get his father's attention, he set King David's fields on fire. It was only after the smoke of his ruined crops reached David's nostrils did he utter the words Absalom most wanted to hear: "I will see you now" (II Samuel 14:28–33).

Isn't much of the frustration of customers that of not being seen? Of being placed in a purgatorium of invisibility while the rest of the world goes on?

I am constantly amazed at how a customer calling from the comfort of their home will almost always receive attention ahead of the customer who has brought herself into the store or office to make face-to-face contact for service. Isn't it true?

One time I waited ten minutes in a line in a department store and, when I finally got to the counter, the phone rang and the service clerk answered, said "Excuse me" to the caller as she put her on hold, and then went to see if they did indeed have chartreuse slippers in her size. AARGH! It happens constantly—in stores—in families—in companies—the frustration of not being seen.

I will never forget a stewardess on Flight 392 to Detroit. It was during an airlines pilot strike, so numerous flights had been canceled. I had the joy of not only getting bumped but having my first-class ticket be good only for coach. The snow was coming down, mixed with sleet, and people were being jammed into this 747 as if it were a 1047 (if there is such an aircraft—which there should be—especially that day!). Since it was such wintry weather, people were bringing their coats onboard, and since the baggage handlers might be the next to strike, people were carrying all their luggage onboard—I mean *all* of it.

Tempers were flaring as I hauled my modest computer case to a coach seat—despite having paid $1,000 extra for a first-class ticket. I was wrestling to get past the other passengers when this lovely Filipino stewardess said, "Oh, my. Let me help you with that." She then turned sweetly to the woman with child behind me and said, "All our overhead bins are full. But put your suitcase over here. You'll be number three." She took the suitcase of a harried businessman and said, "Lucky you! You're number four," and she proceeded to do this with every overluggaged person on the plane—smiling and humming and soothing us as she made eye contact with each passenger and said, "I see you. I won't forget you."

When all that luggage found a place it seemed like a miracle to me. She created a spirit of cooperation and a sense of specialness in each one of us—even though, technically, we were no more than cows to be herded into appropriate stalls.

On a harried, crowded flight, that woman was like an angel. Although she couldn't change our circumstances at the moment, she let us know that we were seen.

Recently, Christ Hospital in Illinois instituted a new program to improve customer satisfaction. It involved a number of complicated process changes, as well as a few very simple ones. Among the simple changes were:

1) Establish eye contact, smile, and say hello to every person you encounter.
2) Before any associate leaves a patient's room, you are to turn and ask, "Is there anything else I can do for you before I go?"

This hospital's scores in customer satisfaction went off the charts with the implementation of these new and simple "I see you" policies, as well as the caring personnel.

They were saying, in essence, to every person they met, "I see you."

Spiritreneurs do that with their customers—with suppliers and coworkers and friends. And especially with family members.

I see you.
I see you.
I'm here.

Like Zaccheus up in a tree, straining to get a glimpse of God, you will be amazed when God turns and smiles and says to you, "Yes—I see you. In fact, let's have dinner in your home tonight" (Luke 19:2–5).

Jesus said, "I see you."

Questions

1. Who are you "not seeing"?
2. Have you ever been overlooked or ignored by someone?
3. Who was it, and how did it make you feel?
4. How can you begin to truly "see" people in your business? Your family?

Dear Lord,
Help me to see others as you see them.
Amen

HE HAD MULTIPLE TITLES

"Are you the King of the Jews?" asked Pilate.
—Matthew 27:11

J esus had the same problem that many spiritreneurs encounter. What should he call himself officially, on his business card? Son of God. Son of Man. King of the Jews. Herod's
nightmare. Mary's boy. Joseph's son. Carpenter Extraordinaire.
Healer.

He had so many titles that one preacher delivered an entire
sermon based solely on Jesus' titles. Among them were:

Branch of the Lord
Triumphant Lion
He who is, who was, and who is to come
Faithful witness, Firstborn from the dead, and Ruler of
    Kings of the earth
The Word
"He was with God in the beginning"
Life . . . The light of men

The true light that gives light to every person
Jesus Christ
Lord

Once you bring the Holy Spirit into your business, all
heaven breaks loose. That is why it's so challenging to try to
describe yourself in a few words on a business card. Ken
Blanchard now calls himself "Chief Spiritual Officer" of the
Blanchard Group. Other new titles in vogue, as reported in
Business Finance magazine, include: Brand Breeder, Creator
of Chaos, E-venture Explorer, Rainmaker, Chief Muckey-
Muck, and She Who Must Be Obeyed.

Kathryn Antonacci, our coworker, once spent fifteen minutes describing her titles to a newcomer. I got up, went to the
restroom, and returned to find her still listing roles.

Doug Coe, the man behind the Washington Prayer break-
fasts, doesn't call himself anything on his business card. He
assumes that the Holy Spirit will reveal to you who he is on a
need-to-know basis.

I remember exchanging business cards with a couple of
Buddhist monks at the First State of the World Forum held in
San Francisco. We'd had a pleasant dinner conversation and
afterward I dutifully whipped out my business card. When I
handed it to them they took it as if I'd given them a piece of my
soul. They each bowed and reverentially held it in two
hands—as if it were a sacred thing. I paused. They bowed
again and said they were honored to make my acquaintance. I
looked again to make sure I hadn't given them a $100 bill by
mistake. They treated my business card as if it represented my
soul—my very purpose and reason for being on earth.

They were right. That piece of paper you give people really should represent your soul.

Pilate wrote a title and put it on the cross; it read, "Jesus, of Nazareth, the King of the Jews." Many of the Jews read this title, for the place where Jesus was crucified was near the city, and it was written in Hebrew, Latin, and Greek. The chief priests of the Jews then said to Pilate, "Do not write 'The King of the Jews' but, 'This man said, I am the King of the Jews.' " Pilate answered, "What I have written, I have written" (John 19:19–22, Revised Standard).

What shall we call you as you hang out for the world to see? Jesus had multiple titles.

Questions

1. What titles do you hold in your company?
2. What titles do you hold most dear?
3. Do you relate to the challenge of identifying a single slot? Why?
4. Would you agree that your title(s) may change as you evolve spiritually?
5. Isn't it kind of fun knowing you can no longer be put in a box or a card?

Dear Lord,
You had many titles. But I desire only one, and that is:
"Yours."
   Truly—"yours."
     Amen

HE NEVER UNDERESTIMATED THE WIDOW'S MITE

Your days of mourning will be over.
—Isaiah 60:20

Jesus stood with his disciples as the people filed into the temple to deposit their offerings. While James and John were watching the parade of the Jewish religious leaders with their finery, Jesus turned his eyes to a woman clothed in rags who quietly dropped her mite into the offering plate and then walked silently away.

"Did you see that?" Jesus said. "I tell you what she gave was worth more than all the show-and-tell finery of the Pharisees and the well-to-do. They make a show of their abundance purely to impress the eyes of man—but she gave me everything she had—and because of that, she is truly blessed" (Mark 12:42).

Widows in Jesus' time were women who had been stripped bare. No longer able to share in their husband's status or wealth, no longer to glory in the ability to give birth, they were like the shadow people left to live out their days in silence and poverty. If widowhood were not such a dreaded state, Naomi would not have been so bereft when "I departed full and Yaweh has brought me back to empty. . . . Shaddai has made me wretched" (Ruth 1:21).

So for Jesus to call attention to a "worthless widow" and state her special status in heaven because of her willingness to give all she had, was a reminder to us all not to underestimate a widow's "might" (as I like to spell the word).

There are spiritual and practical lessons to be gleaned from this. I look at this story and see truth shining everywhere. The first truth is a warning that while the eyes of the world may be on the wealthy and their parades, God's eyes are on the humble. He knows where the true power is . . . the power of a heart stripped bare, the power of a soul releasing its last few pennies to God to say, "Take me. I am yours."

The second lesson is a practical one for our time, because statistically widows will, and do, inherit the world. Consider the following statistics compiled by Lu Dunbar, founder and president of Royal Treasure, a nonprofit organization that assists women with investing their time, talents, and treasures. At some point in their lives, 90 percent of all women are solely responsible for their finances. Women now own 60 percent of all assets in the United States. Thirty years ago women were taught that they would be cared for; today they realize that they will probably need to care for themselves. The intergenerational transfer of finances in the next twenty years will be from $8 to $14 trillion—and women will handle most of it.

Stewardship is a daunting concept, seldom taught in churches. However, many women are discovering the fulfilling adventure of investing in God's work. At a recent Council on Foundations gathering, more than 50 percent of the attendees were women under age fifty.

The other observation I have is that women in this day and age can actually blossom in "widowhood." The kids are gone, the husband's gone, and suddenly the bird whose job it was to guard the nest begins to test and enjoy her wings. Sally thought she had lost everything when she lost her husband through divorce. A homemaker most of her life, she faced a future that seemed empty and bleak. Her son David recounted how he gave his mother *The Path,* and she sat down and not only read the book, but did the exercises. Suddenly it dawned on her that she could combine the two things she loved most—scuba diving and teaching kids the wonders of the world. She started a company doing just that and now is flourishing with more business than she can handle. She told her son excitedly, "I am getting paid to play—I really don't 'work' at all. This is glorious!"

Sally's story is proof that even the most dreaded change can be positive—that in losing your former life you may find a new one.

When a soul, stripped to its essence, puts everything it has into the offering plate—therein will lie its glory.

Arise, shine out, for your light has come, and the glory of Yahweh has risen on you. . . . Look! Though night still covers the earth, and darkness the peoples, on you Yahweh is rising, and over you his glory can be seen.

. . .

Instead of your being forsaken and hated, avoided by everyone, I will make you an object of eternal pride—a source of joy from age to age.

. . .

Your sun will set no more nor will your moon wane, for I will be your everlasting light and your days of mourning will be over.
(Isaiah 60:1–2, 15, 20)

Jesus never underestimated the widow's might.

Questions

1. Where in your life could it be said that you have lost your economic and social standing?
2. Why was Jesus so moved by such a small sum of money?
3. What "funerals" need to take place in your life in order for you to be free? Why?
4. How can you daily practice an emptiness before God?
5. Who ultimately will control 60 percent of the world's wealth?
6. How are you treating those people now?

Dear Lord,
Help me release the pennies I cling to as my security and know that you are my source—my husband—my blessing—my joy. Thank you for keeping your eyes on the poor and needy and not being swayed by perfumed yet empty parades. Help me to see like you—into the hearts of others.
Amen

HE STARTED SMALL

And they found the babe lying in a manger.
—Luke 2:16

A t one time Jesus was no bigger than the dot on this *i*.
The Word, which encompassed all of God's love, became
flesh and dwelt among us—first as an embryo, then a child,
then a man. His impact on the world had nothing to do with his
size.

All great people, ideas, events, and organizations have
small beginnings. One of the things that surprised me the most
about my trip to the Holy Land was how small the territory was
that Jesus really covered.

When we were floating on a boat in the middle of the Sea
of Galilee, we could see Tiberias, Capernaum, Magdala,
Chorazin, Bethsaida, all in one glance. Thirteen miles along
the shore of that sea (which is really a lake), is where Jesus
worked some of his greatest miracles. Such a small area to
have had such incredible significance.

Do not think because you are small in size, in resources, in current influence, that God will not see and bless you.

Phil Knight, founder of the Nike Corporation, started his company with a waffle iron in his kitchen. The founders of Hewlett Packard began their company in a garage. So did Steven Jobs of Apple Computers.

In *Chicken Soup for the Soul at Work,* the story is told of a patriarch who was dying. To determine which of his children would receive the inheritance he said, "Whoever brings me something that can fill this room will be the one I designate as heir."

One of the sons used his savings to purchase as many diamonds as he could. When he spread them out on his father's bed all could see that they did not fill the room.

The other son brought sand. He poured it all over the floor—yet even so the room was not full.

Then in came his daughter. She carried only a candle. She asked them to turn out the lights. Then she quietly struck a match, and the flame sputtered and then burned brightly as light flooded the room.

"Well done," said the father to his faithful daughter. "You shall rule my kingdom."

The tiniest flame can pierce the darkness.

Jesus started small.

Questions

1. Are you feeling intimidated because you are not a huge corporation?

2. Describe the particular darkness in the world that concerns you.

3. How could the work you are doing fill the world with light?

Dear Lord,
Let me always choose to be your light in the world, no matter how small my candle may seem to be.
                                            Amen

HE WAS NICE TO HIS BOSS

*He lived under their authority . . . and increased in
wisdom and stature.*

—Luke 2:51–52

Romans 13:1–5 admonishes us to respect those who are
placed in authority over us. I have had good bosses, and
bad bosses. Even the bad bosses were good in that they either
helped me clarify what kind of work atmosphere I didn't want
or they fired and released me to go on to some other kind of
work that suited me better.

Good bosses recognize that they have a God-given responsibility to nurture and develop their employees. Good bosses
are sensitive to the needs of their workers and are always looking for ways to promote their station in life.

Good employees respect and honor their bosses, serving
them as "unto the Lord." The benefits of this type of behavior are well documented in Scripture, especially in the
case of Nehemiah. Nehemiah's boss gave him a leave of
absence and a draw upon the royal treasury so he could re-

turn to his homeland and rebuild the walls of Jerusalem (Nehemiah 2:17).

Although Nehemiah's heart was stirring him to leave his current profession as cupbearer to the king and become a contractor in Jerusalem, Nehemiah did not let his performance— or his respect for the king—fade away.

Too many people burn their bridges behind them when they leave one place of employment to launch their own business or start down a new path. This is unwise and counterproductive, since your boss's words and influence may follow you for a very long time. In my hometown we had a success story of a young man who apparently really impressed several of his bosses.

Richard Beem sold cellular phones for a living, but what he really wanted to do was play professional golf. In a wise career move, he decided to work in a golf shop at the local country club. Even though it meant taking a pay cut, he reasoned that at least he could be around his passion. He quickly moved from golf shop sales attendant to assistant pro, and his boss took notice of his talent and potential. He helped organize a group of thirty-five sponsors who agreed to cover all of Richard's living and travel expenses for two years on the professional tour. The sponsorship pledged the necessary $45,000, as well as a guaranteed two-year exemption from having to qualify for the PGA. According to an article that ran in the *Washington Post*, Richard's boss from the cellular phone store had traveled to the tournament to be there for emotional support. When Richard won his first major tournament, his former bosses at the country club were elated by Richard's success, even though he was no longer working for them. Richard's consistent attitude of humility in service helped become a launching pad for his dream. Like Nehemiah, he was sent on his way by good, kind, and generous bosses whose ultimate goal was to see him succeed.

If you cannot speak well of your boss, you shouldn't be working there. And if you are working there, you should always speak well of your boss. One of the things the Lord hates is "dissembling lips" (Proverbs 12:22).

Dissembling lips are those that are attempting to "disassemble" the very structure currently supporting them. How foolish can that be?

I once knew a man named Don who was working for his father-in-law, Jim. Jim had made many concessions to get— and keep—his son-in-law employed with the company. Don had not held a steady job for ten years.

Yet every word out of his mouth about his father-in-law was how stupid he was, how he couldn't run a business, etc. The effect of his words only caused me to lose respect for Don, who couldn't see that he was hammering away at the very scaffold that was supporting him.

How far can someone get hammering on their own foot? Would you hire someone like that? Would you promote them?

We are cautioned in Scripture to be cautious about criticizing the king, "because a bird will sprout wings and carry your criticisms to him" (Ecclesiastes 10:20). To honor and serve those above you will only cause them to lift you higher. It worked for Nehemiah, and Joseph, and Jacob, and Jesus.

Jesus was nice to his boss.

Questions

1. Are you currently working for a good boss, or a bad one?
2. Do you always speak well of your boss?
3. Does your boss know your big dream? If so, why should he or she care about helping you?
4. Have you honestly been helping your boss to accomplish his or her dreams and goals?

Dear Lord,

Help me serve others as if I were serving you, for, in all things I do, I ultimately am serving you. Thank you for the good boss and bosses who have helped me get this far.

Amen

THE LURCH: THE EARLY DAYS AND YOUR NEW IDENTITY

One does not have to read far in Scripture to realize that "challenge" is God's middle name. The Garden of Eden you've been placed in during your exuberant Launch has a serpent smack dab in the middle of it. You disobey your marching orders and suddenly you are on your own—in brambles and quicksand and trouble.

Or perhaps your Lurch comes not through a willful act of disobedience, but a sudden turn of events. You are doing everything you've been told to do, but for some unknown reason the doors just aren't swinging open anymore. In fact, Pharaoh is chasing you and, man, is he ever mad.

Perhaps your peers don't understand and try to have you thrown off a cliff, as happened to a young Jesus shortly after he performed his first few miracles. "And the people said, 'Get away from here,' and took him out to a cliff."

Or maybe you are like the young King David, still flush from having slain Goliath, who is shocked when your benefactor turns against you and hurls a spear at your head. "So much for God's anointing," you cry as you grab what you can and jump over the palace wall, where you spend the next fifteen years or so begging for food, picking up renegade employees, and mingling with people you used to consider beneath you. One day you even find yourself pretending to be a madman so your captors will let you go.

The Lurch is where the promise gets tested—goes underground, and seems to disappear. The Lurch is where you realize that this journey is not going to be a cakewalk—no matter who your relatives are. The Lurch is where you begin to question if you have done the right thing at all. The Lurch is where you are shaken to your very bones.

Whereas during the Launch you would awaken in the middle of night to excitedly jot down your revelations, in this phase you wake up at 2:00 A.M. wondering why you have jeopardized your family, your career, your sanity.

The only game you seem to play now is "credit card Monopoly" as you shuffle the shiny plastic cards, trying to determine which one will help you make payroll. "It wasn't God that brought me here," you think. "It must have been the Devil." The biggest accomplishment of your day is getting your frequent customer card stamped at the local coffee shop.

Every spiritreneur encounters this phase. So did Jesus.

Imagine his feelings when the crowds who had seen the dove descend on him after he was baptized by John refused to believe what he was saying. People who were supposed to be his friends became enemies. The start date on his business plan was pushed forward by his insistent mother. People he told not to say anything went blabbing to everyone in town. He went back to his home village to share his many gifts, and their doubts prevented him from performing even one miracle.

The Lurch. Every spiritreneur goes through it. This section is designed to encourage you, and to let you know that if you persevere, you will survive.

HE KNEW HE COULDN'T QUIT

*For the very work the Father has given me to finish
testifies that He sent me.*

—John 5:36

Eight-year-old Antonio decided to build a tree house in my
backyard. Always eager to encourage enterprise in children, I dutifully got out the necessary hammer, nails, saw,
boards, and measuring tape. He worked alone for a few hours,
came in and got some cookies, and then went back outside.
Soon, however, he encountered a few obstacles. His six-year-
old cousin Joseph insisted on helping him. His four-year-old
cousin Jacob started carrying off the nails one by one and
putting them in a hole he had dug over by the rose garden.
Joshua, the "circus dog," kept climbing up the slanted trunk
to lick Antonio in the ear as he was working, while Miguel, his
twelve-year-old brother, began telling him his tree house
looked dumb. Gabriela, his ten-year-old sister, told him the
floorboard was tilted too far to the left.

When Antonio couldn't find the right-sized board for his
window because Joseph was using it to paint a "Dinosaur exit"

sign, his patience wore thin. He came into the sunroom, threw down his hammer, and said, "Laurie, you can't pay me enough to build that tree house! I quit!"

I sat back and waited for him to calm down. Then I said, "Antonio, building the tree house was your idea. You can't quit, because nobody else hired you—you hired yourself!"

"Oh yeah," he said, sitting down. "Bummer." Eventually he went back outside, picked up his hammer, and headed off determined to complete the job.

I remember a similar lesson as my mother sat me down to go over the books of my first enterprise, Jesse Jones Promotions. I was dumbfounded as she explained that the company—which was me—owed the other me (the individual) money, but because the company me had made a capital contribution, the money the company me owed the other me wouldn't balance unless a third me loaned the other me more money.

"How many me's are there is this company anyway?" I asked.

"Honey, I've been asking myself that same question," she said as she looked at the figures.

Like Antonio I was ready to shout, "You can't pay me enough to build this tree house. I quit!" And I have felt like saying it many times since.

Not too long ago, in fact, I had a spell where everything I put my hand to was turning to mud. To top it off, I had developed a, shall we say, poor attitude about work. As my administrator Dee was explaining some corrections she'd made to take care of my errors, I sighed and said, "Dee, if I didn't work for me I'd fire me right now." She laughed and encouraged me to take an entire week off.

"Don't open the mail. Don't answer the phone. And for Pete's sake, don't make any decisions right now. I'll watch the fort. You go play with your horses."

Which is exactly what I did.

Having no boss but yourself as a spiritreneur is a two-edge sword. Nobody can fire you. That's the good news. But then, there's nobody else to blame when things go wrong. That's the bad news.

People who work for someone else seem to always have the luxury of complaining about how things are done at the top. When the Israelites, who had been slaves for four hundred years, were suddenly set free to the land of spiritreneurhood, it is little wonder that many of them wanted to go back.

Like the Israelites, spiritreneurs leave the slave chains but become aware of other sounds at night. "Was that a lion coughing in the background? How close are they?" were questions the Israelites never had to ask themselves in Egypt. "They worked us hard, but at least we got fed."

A spiritreneur's circumstance is that s/he not only has to row the boat but also has to trim the sail, swab the deck, haul the water, feed the crew, and steer the ship—sometimes in no particular order. The spiritreneur is the galley slave *and* the slave guard.

One of my business owner friends said once that there are days when she envies the garbage collectors. "How relaxing it must be to know exactly what you were supposed to be doing each minute of your workday," she sighed. It is the deciding, the prioritizing, the adjusting, the constant steering that keeps spiritreneurs awake at night. Who fears a mean boss when there are sharks watching you?

My friend Linda and her husband, Lee, bought a 40-foot sailboat and lived aboard it for five years. They sailed from Alaska to Mexico and back again; they had both beautiful days and stormy weather. When I asked Linda what was the most terrifying moment she experienced, she said it was during a rough passage south. It was a moonlit night and a storm had come up. The waves were rising thirty feet behind them. She was on the midnight-to-2:00-A.M. watch, steering the *Argonaut* ever onward while Lee was asleep in the hold.

She said, "I had my safety harness on and was doing my best to keep a steady course, when suddenly the hair on the back of my neck stood up and I felt this terrible sense of danger." She turned and there—looking right at her in the midst of a 30-foot wave—was a great white shark.

"Laurie, that wave was rising up behind me and I turned and looked right into his eyes. I screamed and Lee came stumbling up out of the hold, but by then the shark had gone under. Lee thought I must have been imagining things until we finally got to port and other sailors reported seeing similar things on moonlit nights in high seas. One couple actually had a wave crash onto their boat—delivering an 80-pound octopus onto their ship."

"What did they do?" I asked.

Lee laughed. "They called out, 'All hands on deck!' and threw the thing overboard."

As sailors, Lee and Linda caught their own fish, hauled their own water. Linda made awnings for other boats. They ate fresh vegetables from the market.

How rich were Linda and Lee in those days? You probably have more in your bank account than they did then. But oh, I considered them by far the wealthiest couple I knew. And no matter how high the waves got, Lee and Linda didn't quit.

"Set sail! Set sail! Why are your boats still in the harbor?" cried Deborah to the tribes of Israel (Judges 5:15–17). The boats were in the harbor because they were afraid.

Spiritreneurs begin adventures that will often have fear as a lurking companion. But the important thing is to continue on the course that you have set.

Jesus knew he couldn't quit.

Questions

1. Do you have what it takes to be your own boss? What do you think it might entail?
2. Which would you rather see—a shark behind you on a moonlit night or a row of sweaty backs in front of you, doing the same thing over and over and over?
3. What other spiritreneurs in the Bible wanted to say, "I quit!"?

Dear Lord,
Building a tree house seemed like such a good idea at one time. Help me to overcome all the obstacles to see it through to completion. Remind me, rekindle in me the enthusiasm I first had when the tree branches beckoned me. Let me never trade in my hammer for a remote control.
Amen

HE KNEW IT WAS OK TO LIMP TO THE FINISH LINE

The sun rose as he passed Peniel, limping from his hip.

—Genesis 32:32

In our culture we are so obsessed with appearances that some people would rather die than "fail." People who leap off balconies or put a bullet through their heads are, in some ways, saying, "I don't want to be seen as a failure, so I'd rather not be seen at all."

Thirty- and sixty-second commercials that show muddy clothes being instantly transformed to whiter than white convey the message that if you just find—and use—the right product, all your problems will disappear. Our "success stories," which emphasize the glorious finish, communicate that winners—in the end—are always balanced, perfect, and poised.

Wall Street wants tidy answers and hefty profits—spare us the details of how you got there. Make it up and make it quick—and leave no witnesses to tell the bloody tales of who and what was sacrificed to get there.

Yet, a spiritreneur must recognize that we can't always look good while we're getting there. We cannot postpone media attention until all our carefully hired and trained characters are in place—having memorized their lines, starched their shirts, and used Pepsodent besides.

Perhaps we all still suffer from the illusion that a long-legged bird drops off the babies, already diapered, at the front door. Spiritreneurs know otherwise, and are willing to accept the reality that babies are often born in a screaming bloody mess, sometimes coming out backwards, sometimes coming too soon.

I remember hearing Bill Pollard, CEO of ServiceMaster, speak about his four-billion-dollar company. As he took the podium to share his pearls of wisdom with us, he smiled and said, "Hello. I'm Bill Pollard, CEO of a company with 250,000 employee associates. Our mission is to honor God, develop people, pursue excellence, and grow profitably. And the one thing I can guarantee you is that even as I stand here, somewhere someone of our employees is messing up." There was a burst of laughter from the crowd. This titan of success was real. He continued, "And after I leave this lovely gathering and board our corporate jet, I know that when I arrive at my next destination my task will be to mop up the mistake and try to make it right. I go from microphones to mops on a daily basis."

ServiceMaster. Four billion dollars of revenues generated annually by people making mistakes—mopping them up, and doing better the next time.

The bugaboo of spiritreneurs is perfectionism, supported by an ego that always wants to look good. I remember working for three years to attain the presidency of a local group in San Diego. The man I was succeeding was a polished, crisp-white-shirt, thousand-dollar-suit insurance executive who exuded confidence and control. As God would have it, we met in the elevator going up to my first official presiding meeting.

This group met in La Jolla, California, at 7:16 A.M. every Tuesday, which meant I always had to dress in the predawn darkness to get there on time. This particular day, I was primed—black Tahari dress, appropriate brooch, stunning black pumps.

"Good morning, Troy!" I smiled as we stepped onto the elevator together.

"Good morning, Laurie," he said cheerily. "You're looking mighty fine today, as always."

"You too, sir." I nodded politely, already mentally rehearsing my inaugural address.

Nothing was said for a few seconds and then Troy cleared his throat and said softly, "I see you have a little trailer there."

I glanced down at my feet and in horror discovered I was dragging a pair of pantyhose out of my left shoe. (I always stuff the appropriate color into the appropriately colored shoes the night before.) I hurriedly lifted my foot and yanked the offending hose out just as the door opened and the welcoming committee rushed to greet me.

The one man I had most wanted to impress, the highly popular and efficient outgoing president, had seen me already at my inefficient worst. "She can't even dress herself and she's going to run this club?" he might have been thinking as he ceremoniously handed me the gavel. Trailing pantyhose notwithstanding, the gavel was passed to me and my "reign" began. And thus I limped across the finish line.

My favorite biblical example of this is the story about Jacob, a man who had ambition oozing out of every pore. "And then Jacob was left alone. Someone wrestled with him until daybreak who, seeing that he could not master him, struck him on the hip socket, and Jacob's hip was dislocated as he wrestled with him. He said, 'Let me go, for day is breaking.' Jacob replied, 'I will not let you go unless you bless me.' The other said, 'What is your name?' 'Jacob,' he replied. He said, 'No longer are you to be called Jacob but Israel, since you have shown your strength against God and men and have prevailed.' Then Jacob asked, 'Please tell me your name.' He replied, 'Why do you ask my name?' With that, he blessed him there. Jacob named the place Peniel, 'Because I have seen God face to face,' he said, 'and have survived.' The sun rose as he passed Peniel, limping from his hip. That is why to this day the Israelites do not eat the thigh sinew which is at the hip socket: because he had struck Jacob there" (Genesis 32:22–32).

I think about this story a lot for us spiritreneurs. Anyone who endeavors to scale the ladder to heaven encounters powerful forces along the way. A bankruptcy, perhaps. A failed relationship. A scent of fear even as the fireworks go off. A mop at the microphone. Those who persist and never give up will be blessed—even though they may limp after the encounter.

In Silicon Valley failure is almost seen as a badge of honor. Ousted CEOs usually have multiple job offers awaiting them simply because they have demonstrated, like Jacob, the ability to survive.

Do not think you can wrestle with powers larger than your own and remain unscathed. The story of Jacob is there to remind us that it is OK with God if we limp to the finish line.

Jesus certainly did.

Questions

1. Where are you trying too hard to look good, rather than *be* good?
2. What forces are you currently wrestling with?
3. What new name might you be given as a result of your divine wrestling match?
4. Why do you think God didn't allow Jacob just to take a magic carpet ride to his blessings?
5. Are you letting your "limp" keep you from crossing the finish line?

Oh Lord, thank you for wrestling with me . . . for testing my arms and my stamina and my will to see if I really am strong enough—determined enough—to climb to heaven's store. Take the hard places in and under my head and use them to convey your visions of glory. Let me shout my new name with glee even as I limp to the finish line, for surely, just as you promised Jacob, your blessings await me.

Amen

HE SAID, "DID YOU LOOK UP ON THE ROOF?"

I will lift up mine eyes to the hills, from whence cometh my help.

—Psalms 121:1

After the piñata party was over, I surveyed the damage. It seemed minimal considering there had been ten children present, ranging in age from three to twelve. The last of the candy and shredded paper had been distributed or put away. Paper plates and party favors were all properly deposited. Only as I began to close up the ranch for the night did I notice that the iron latch to the entrance gate was missing. I did a thorough search of the premises, and when nothing turned up, I placed a call to eight-year-old Antonio—the one to whom all turn when something seems out of the ordinary. "Antonio," I said gently, "the gate latch is missing. Do you know anything about it?"

"Oh, how silly," he said nonchalantly, as I heard him sip his soda. "Did you look up on the roof?"

I was so stunned at his perspective that I had to laugh. "Of course, why didn't I think of that?" I said, thanking him as I hung up the phone.

And there, between the air conditioner and the rain gutter, lay the latch to the gate.

As spiritreneurs we must look where others fail to look—for answers, for solutions, for opportunities. The world is a mystical, magical place, and abundance is everywhere.

An embarrassed and distraught disciple came running up to Jesus. "Uh, Master, we're in trouble with the TTB [Temple Tax Bureau]. It seems we haven't paid our taxes, and penalties and interest are accruing rapidly."

"Oh how silly," Jesus seemed to say. "Did anybody look in the fish's mouth?" There the troubled staffer found a gold coin which was more than enough to pay for the tax (Matthew 17:24–27).

"We can't get in. There's no way. The crowd is blocking the doors," whispered one of the desperate men. "And, if we don't get in to see him tonight, we might not get to see him at all. I hear he's leaving tomorrow!" There was a long pause as the men thought about what to do.

"I guess it's hopeless," said the older, more experienced man, as he instructed his friends to lift up the litter holding their comrade.

"I've got an idea," said a little girl watching. "Why not go in through the roof?"

Jesus, the seminar speaker, saw a foot crashing through the plaster-and-mud ceiling and then, lowered slowly down, an ill man with some very, very good friends.

"Master, will you heal him?" they asked.

And the Master said, "I shall" (Mark 2:4).

Spiritreneurs never give up. If we can't get in through the door, we'll go in through the roof.

One key characteristic of spiritreneurs is that we don't just believe money grows on trees—we believe it can sprout up from anywhere. Like Jesus found a gold coin in a fish's mouth, perhaps. Or Elijah discovered food in a raven's beak (1 Kings 17:4–6). Or the quail on the wing that Moses caught for the Israelites (Numbers 11:32).

When spiritreneurs are on a mission, we will find sustenance and support from the most unlikely places. Indeed, it is this confidence that the money is there (or will be) that can drive other people crazy.

When I decided to drop out of college to pursue my writing career my father instructed my mother to cut off my cash flow. I'd expected that, but then I felt as if God had hired me to write, so He would be my source now, not my dad. Amazing things happened for me during that time. I'd be walking down the street by a park and find a $20 bill on the sidewalk— with no one in sight. I met a man on a plane trip back from Atlanta who wrote out a $500 check on the spot to cover my month's rent.

Ahh. I sigh remembering those days. I don't ever want to go back to them exactly, those days of daily praying for my daily bread, but the experience deepened my faith and strengthened my resolve. It proved to me that there are many streams in the desert, and you just never know when—or how—a blessing will turn up.

I remember a particularly trying time. I was worse than unemployed. I was deeply in debt. My real estate investments had turned from cash cows into alligators. My advertising clients had dried up as well during the recession, and I had just signed a personal note to repay a $100,000 investment that had gone sour. My book *Jesus, CEO* was already launched but the advance money wasn't going to cover my debts—most of which had been run up while I quit working to write the book.

The first two drafts of my next book had been rejected by my agent, and I was beginning to wonder how I'd make a living now—no new book, no rental income, no clients.

I went to visit my mother in Sedona, who lovingly assured me that yes, I could not live there, and with a very contemplative heart I went for a walk down a gulley, which wound through the hills. Mom had told me just the night before that last year there had been a sudden spring rain that sent a gully washer down that empty creek bed—a gully washer so high that one woman had to be evacuated from the roof of her home.

I thought about that as I walked along, praying about the future. Suddenly I heard a voice say, "Laurie, do you see this dried-up creek bed?"

"Yes," I said, "I'm walking in it."

"Do you believe that I can cause it to overflow with water at my command?"

"Yes, I know you can. You flooded it last spring."

"Well, just keep walking. Your footsteps may seem like they are on sand but I will cause your finances to flow suddenly—in ways beyond measure."

My heart leapt up in recognition and acceptance, and a peace came over me. I returned home to find Mom in the kitchen, preparing a chicken salad.

"Did you and the Lord figure out your future?" she asked.

"Yes, we did," I said.

She smiled knowingly and kept cutting up chicken. "Ready to try again on a third draft of your book?" she asked.

"Yes." I smiled. "I'm ready to write. Got any blank paper?"

And I sat there in Sedona with a song in my heart and wrote out a third draft, which my agent accepted, and forty-five days later we signed a publishing contract for more money than I had ever seen in my life. The first payment arrived almost one year to the day of the spring flood in Sedona. The Lord did indeed send me a gully washer.

"I can't seem to find my financial source, Lord," you might be saying.

"Oh, how silly," Jesus replies.

"Have you looked up on the roof?"

Jesus looked up on the roof.

Questions

1. Where are you looking for your financial security?
2. Who—or what—do you really see as your source?
3. Do you see opportunities everywhere, or do you give up at the first hint of a rejection?
4. Can you think of times in your life where help suddenly appeared out of nowhere?

Dear Lord,
Take me up on the roof. Let me see the stars and escape the
dirt that seems to bind me to the earth. Let's play hide-
and-seek, Dear God—and I will look until I find you.

Amen

HE SAW THE ARMY

And behold, the mountain was full of horses and chariots.

—2 Kings 6:16

One of my favorite stories in Scripture is that of a young frightened Israelite king who feared losing a battle. The prophet Elisha prayed that the veil of heaven would be lifted and that the desperate king would see the forces of heaven gathered there to help him.

And Elisha said, "Lord, I pray thee, open his eyes that he may see." And the Lord opened the eyes of the young man, and he saw; and behold the mountain was full of horses, and chariots of fire stood round about Elisha. And he answered, "Fear not, for they that be with us are more than they that be with them" (2 Kings 6:16–17).

This vision gave the king courage, and he prevailed. Recently I was in New York talking with an enthusiastic young spiritreneur, a former "rocker" and factory worker who had walked out of a party one night, gazed up at the stars, and said, "God, if you're real, show me. If not, I'll keep partying." It wasn't long before the gnawing in his heart caused him to go back to church. His studies there led him to a desire to become a full-time pastor. He now has a church in New York with seventy-five members, each of whom was radiant and joyful when they attended my book signing party. I asked him, "So, Pastor Sal, where did you get your theological training?"

"On my face," he said and laughed. I laughed with him as I realized the significance of his words. "God seems to teach me best in the spiritual boxing ring," he said, "and I always lose."

Then he turned and motioned to his congregation members. "These people keep lifting me up and pushing me out in front of them. I can't tell if they love me or hate me." He chuckled.

"We're his army" said one of the members. "We just don't wear a uniform." I looked at Sal and his wife, Dana, and marveled at how rich he is. I had a sense that this group would stand with him and for him. Or, if need be, lift him up off his face after another round with God. I realized that in dealing with Sal, I wasn't just dealing with him, but with the seventy-five business executives and moms and youth leaders and little kids who loved him.

We are never truly alone, although at times we feel like we are. As I was walking through the streets of New York after seeing Sal, dodging taxis as they swept past me, splashing rainwater on my feet, I thought of all the people walking the streets with me that day. People who were hoping to get hired as an actor or actuary or stockbroker or consultant based on their portfolio . . . black leather cases filled with plastic sheets detailing their references and their accomplishments, which pointed to a bright and wonderful future. I remembered so often knocking on doors trying to gain entry into a kingdom of my desiring. (After one particular job interview with a prestigious law firm, I got up, turned, and walked into the coat closet.)

Do you feel alone right now? Are you feeling like a student "without portfolio"—wandering the cold wet streets of a city that doesn't know your name and doesn't seem to want to?

Picture this, then. You are related to King David, the kid who was anointed king at the age of eleven and finally succeeded in ruling the known kingdom of God. You are a blood relative to Joseph, the man whose foresight saved the world from famine. You have in your gallery of relatives Queen Esther, who risked her life and her crown to save an entire race from destruction. You are blood relatives to the fisherman who shouldered through hostile crowds to meet the man who would change history, the man who could stand up and shake all the stars out of his lap and create universes and galaxies and supernovas without measure.

"May I see your references?" asks the frowning face behind the desk. Then you smile and say like Moses, "Yes of course, but you may want to shield your eyes first, for an incredible army of the Lord is about to pass by."

Jesus saw the army.

Questions

1. Describe the battle that you feel you are losing right now.
2. Imagine looking up and seeing the army of God surrounding you.
3. How do you feel now?

Dear Lord,
Help me see your army. Help me lift my head in certainty
and power, and shoulder on to prevail.
                                        Amen

HE HEEDED THE
"NOT SHALT" RULE

If you are the Son of God turn these stones into bread.
—Matthew 4:1–3

And Jesus, full of the Holy Spirit, returned from the Jordan, and was led by the Spirit for forty days in the wilderness, tempted by the devil. And he ate nothing in those days . . . and he was hungry" (Luke 4:1–2).

Jesus was in a vulnerable state out there in the wilderness. He was hungry. He was alone. He was tired. The Devil even tried to make him angry as well, hoping this would set him off. Jesus did not act during this state of mind, other than to say no, and "Get away from me." He held his temper, his emotions, his hunger in check, and as a result we all are blessed.

A friend of mine who was twenty years sober once shared with me a guideline for decision making I will never forget. I was in a very low space emotionally, having just lost my father to a heart attack. I wasn't sleeping well, and my diet consisted of a Dr. Pepper for breakfast, a Dr. Pepper for lunch, and

Mexican food for dinner. I couldn't understand why I kept getting the shakes in the afternoon (and I don't mean vanilla).

I was about to decide to make a major geographical move as well, when my friend said, "Laurie, I think I need to share with you the NOT SHALT rule I learned in AA."

"What's that—thou shalt not drink?" I asked.

"No," she replied, "it's an acronym. You should never make a decision when you are

Sad
Hungry
Angry
Lonely or
Tired."

I have used this acronym many times in my business and consulting work since. It is a very wise rule.

Last night as I was thinking about this my mind was suddenly filled with stories in Scripture where people did not follow the NOT SHALT rule and suffered for it.

In her grief over losing her husband and two sons, Naomi foresaw only death and destruction in her future, even though God had Ruth, the daughter-in-law who pledged lifelong loyalty, standing right by her side.

Naomi forgot about God when she was sad (Ruth 1:11–18).

Hungry Esau might have ruled Israel if he hadn't sold his birthright to Jacob for a bowl of stew. "What good is a birthright to a starving man?!" he exclaimed as he sold his rights away to a more clever, and full, Jacob. Esau acted foolishly when he was hungry (Genesis 25:32).

Moses angrily killed an Egyptian guard who was mistreating an Israelite slave, and as a result was banished from Egypt for forty years. Saul got angry at David for his success, and his ill-temper cost him the throne.

David was feeling a little lonely when he met Bathsheba. He was strolling alone in the evening on his roof when he noticed this beautiful woman taking a bath. He thought she might make a great companion for the night, and in so doing brought tragedy to many people. David messed up when he was lonely.

The Israelites were tired. They were tired of walking in circles in the desert. They were tired of eating that manna and quail combination which seemed to be the only thing on the menu. They were tired of waiting for Moses, who had gone up into the clouds supposedly to talk to God. So they took matters into their own hands and started building a god that they could see—one they could make dance to their own tunes and their own pace. The Israelites really made God mad by making dumb decisions when they were tired.

Scripture is full of examples of people who acted when they were sad, hungry, angry, lonely, or tired, and ended up suffering because of it.

I have seen—and perhaps you have, too—businesses, families, friendships destroyed because of a word spoken or a decision made outside the NOT SHALT rule.

A lonely husband on the road decides to seek companionship for just one night, and ends up losing his entire family. A sad teenager, rejected by a girlfriend, takes a gun and shoots himself and other innocent people. A hungry CEO leverages the company too much in order to purchase that jewel of a holding, and doing so brings about the collapse of both of them. An angry daughter says words to her mother that cut her to the bone. All of these could have been avoided if the person in question had been aware of their mental, emotional, or physical state before they acted.

Jesus was tired. Sometimes he was sad. Or angry. He even experienced hunger and loneliness, just as we do. Yet, Jesus obeyed the "NOT SHALT" rule.

Questions

1. Name three other people in Scripture or history in general who violated the NOT SHALT rule and suffered for it.
2. Can you name a specific time when you made a poor decision? Were any of the SHALT elements present? If so, which ones?
3. What can you do to avoid making decisions in less than optimum circumstances?

Dear Lord,
Help me remember the "NOT SHALT" rule for decision making. Help me always seek to maintain a well-fed, well-rooted body, mind, and spirit. Give me good company, and an even temper, so that all my decisions may reflect your wisdom and glory.

Amen

HE WAS IN OVER HIS HEAD

It is by faith you stand.
—2 Corinthians 1:24

In the Garden of Gethsemane Jesus came to the end of his rope. With no easy answers on the horizon, he had come to the limit of all his human mind knew. All he could do was proceed by faith.

It recently occurred to me that the people I find most interesting are those who admit they are in over their head. By this I mean that they are engaged in activities that lie beyond their comfort level and their obvious areas of expertise. Unable to see the shore clearly, they are required to navigate by faith.

In a roundtable conversation I had with several spiritreneurs, the common theme expressed was that they were in their current occupations only by the grace of God, and were forced daily to rely on faith and prayer to get them through. Seated at the table with me were a CEO of a health care system employing 15,000 people, a neurosurgeon, a bank president, and a nun who had just launched a spirituality center for the region. Each one of them admitted that their daily modus operandi was turning decisions over to God in trust.

Perhaps many of us grew up thinking that, no matter what the question, somebody would always know the answer. Only as we become adults did we realize that many questions cannot be "answered." We are left to pursue them by faith.

Not too long ago my administrator and I trekked to the top of the mountain to meet with a man who would surely point us in the right direction as our organization began to expand. A well-known business consultant and author who has attained an enviable level of success, he, we were certain, would be able to give us words of wisdom. When we arrived he and his leading advisor greeted us with, "We are so glad you're here! We were hoping you could help point us in the right direction." We sat down with a stunned look on our faces and finally admitted that the reason we had come was to seek guidance from them. His advisor shook his head and broke into a smile at the irony of our mutual requests. He then looked around the group and said, "Well then, we only have one solution, don't we? Let us pray." With that we all put our heads down and prayed, realizing that we were in over our heads.

As spiritreneurs we are constantly marching into the unknown. I refer often to the vision in Ezekiel 47 about the stream that flows from the tabernacle. At first Ezekiel is able to stand in it. Soon, however, he is led deeper "until it reached his knees." And not long after that it is a river so deep he is no longer able to stand.

To me this signifies the spiritual journey. We begin with the basics of what we know—that God is good, that we are loved, that we are called into service—and pretty soon after that, we're yelling, "Help, I'm drowning!" as the territory becomes unfamiliar and the landmarks are speeding by too fast. Quickly the river of truth and blessing carries us beyond our control.

Even Jesus experienced the feeling of being overwhelmed at times. He could turn a bottle of water into a jug of wine without so much as batting an eye. But as the crowds grew thicker and the stakes got higher, we begin to realize that he too was having to draw on faith. As he approached the garden to pray he knew he was getting in over his head. He wept and prayed in his humanness that the cup would be passed from him. Every cell in his body, every synapse in his brain was screaming, "Don't do this!" Yet somehow, with faith he was able to complete the task that was set before him. When he cried, "Into your hands I commit my spirit," he was admitting that he was not in control—that he was trusting a Higher Power to take over for him in the hour of his death.

We are, all of us, in over our heads. Those who realize it are truly the only ones who have power.

David once cried in despair, "These people are too much for me." So did Moses, Elijah, Jeremiah. The Bible is full of stories about people who admitted that they were in over their heads.

So where shall we turn when there are no answers? "I wake up every day," Marsha Casey, the CEO who leads 15,000, says, "and I pray that God will guide every step I take. And then at noon I pray again. And at three, and at five, and at six."

"Not my will, but thine" (Luke 22:42).

Jesus was in over his head.

Questions

1. Are you in over your head?
2. Do you feel that you are losing or have lost control?
3. What landmarks have disappeared?

Dear Lord,

Help. I have sailed off the map. I see no horizon. I cannot feel the ground beneath my feet. Come to me walking on the water, and lead my ship safely home.

Amen

HE KNEW HE COULD CRY
IF HE WANTED TO

Jesus wept.
    —John 11:35

I grew up hearing Leslie Gore's song coming over the radio, "It's my party and I'll cry if I want to . . ." If you're a baby boomer you could probably recite most of the words with me. The situation described in the song is that of a young girl who throws a birthday party, only to have the boy she loves reject her and walk out with someone else. She says through her tears that she can cry if she wants to, if for no other reason than she paid for the balloons.

For some reason that song reminds me of Jesus on one of his really down days. He, too, had come to earth in a celebration, and to have his lover Israel reject him so continuously literally brought him to tears.

"Oh Jerusalem, Jerusalem how oft I would have gathered you under my wings, but you would have none of me . . ." and so, Jesus wept (Matthew 23:37).

As a spiritreneur I can relate somewhat to that feeling—the feeling of being so rejected and misunderstood that all you can do is cry.

At times like these—go ahead and cry. It is, after all, your party.

Recently I was conversing with a psychologist from Berkeley who was speculating on the interest people have these days in the subject of past lives. This doctor theorized that we seek to know more about the past than we do the future, because the human soul loves drama and surprise. Few of us really want to know what is going to happen in our future because that would take all the fun out of the party. Tony Robbins asks his seminar participants, "What is the story of your life? A soap opera? A romance? A comedy? An action adventure?" What do you want it to be?

One woman went from victim to volunteer. Constance had known physical and verbal abuse as a child, so even when she began her career in real estate she made time to volunteer with some of East Los Angeles's at-risk youth. As she was tutoring them she noticed that all the schools shut down at 5 P.M.—leaving the children no place to congregate at night or on weekends. So, she gathered up $50,000 of her own savings, rented an empty building in the heart of a gang-related area, and opened up a place called At Home, where kids could gather away from street corners and the influence of gangs. The rules for membership in the At Home club were simple: no guns, no drugs, no racist or sexist comments, no gang colors. And the children began to come.

Here they are mentored by volunteers, taught computer and

job-finding skills, tutored in math and English, taught conflict resolution and basic life skills. Last year At Home had 2,000 members—all former or potential gang bangers. Constance could have cried about her life if she wanted to. But she decided to lay out a banquet instead.

Jesus did the same.

As spiritreneurs we have each been given incredible gifts. If we have lived at all, we've also endured pain. Sometimes when we are about to have the greatest breakthrough, we find ourselves on the verge of breakdown.

When I realized the enormity of the gap between where I was as an advertising agency owner and where I wanted to be as a free-form spiritreneur, I went home to be with my mother. Usually we take walks holding hands and then pull up a chair on the back porch, sip a glass of iced tea, and philosophize for hours. This time, however, I got off the plane, saw her face—and began to cry. I always tear up when I first see my mother, but this time I couldn't stop crying. In fact, I cried for three solid days. I cried as I went into the utility room to get out the measuring tape. I cried as I walked out to the backyard, stepping off the space between the chinaberry tree and the cottonwood tree to see if there would be room for me to park a mobile home there. I was almost certain that my newfound path in the forest was going to take me through the woods of bankruptcy, and I at least wanted to know that I'd have a place to live.

Mom said, "Honey, what are you doing?" I just shook my head and kept measuring. Finally, as the Easter weekend drew to a close, Mom said, "Laurie, you have to go back now." I shook my head and began to cry again.

"Honey, you have two business partners and five employees who are depending on you for leadership." At this point I began to wail. "I can't face them! I can't face them, Mom! I'm going to have to tell all of them good-bye." She shook her head, then stood up, extending her hand. "If that's what you have to do, God will give you the strength to do it. Now come on. It's time to go catch your plane."

I wept as I walked down that long, long aisle to the airplane because the party I had created up till now was about to be over.

You, too, may find yourself crying at your own party . . . not because someone has rejected you, but because you now have to say, "This party is over. And a new one is about to begin."

Life as a spiritreneur isn't easy.

Jesus knew he could cry if he wanted to.

Questions

1. Do you feel a lump in your throat as you face the changes that are now facing you?

2. Can you give yourself permission to cry through the problem, just as Jesus did in the Garden of Gethsemane?

3. As a spiritreneur, I acknowledge I want my life, from now on, to be:
   a) An action adventure
   b) A romantic comedy
   c) An epic tale of heroic courage
   d) An inspiration to thousands
   e) A banquet
   f) All of the above

Dear Lord,
Crying came with your territory, and it has certainly come
with mine. Please turn my breakdown into a break-
through, and turn my tears into joy—the joy of loving,
knowing, and expressing you more.

Amen

HE KNEW A BUSINESS PLAN
WOULDN'T SAVE HIM

For where there is no vision, the people perish.
—Prov 29:18

Sitting on my desk are numerous business plans that people have sent me to review. Two of them weigh four pounds each. One of them has so many tab dividers it looks like placards at a political convention. The other has so many trademark, copyright, and service symbols after each word that I feel after reading it I should apply for the witness protection program. Another plan I received today is from a Native American, who simply sent a photograph of himself in costume and twenty letters of reference. Yet another plan consists of a single page, with two product samples attached. The plan I've spent considerable time looking at is a twenty-page fax, full of typos such as "A current trend of *not* that we are considering . . ." This plan is one of two plans I have commissioned sophisticated businesspeople to write for me. The other one, which weighed about eight pounds and cost many thousands of dollars, is somewhere in storage—either here, or in San Diego. Never let it be said that I did not, at least, have a business plan. Now, ask me where it is and I'll have to think a minute.

Of the business plans mentioned above, which one do you think will succeed? As you think about your answer, let me share with you the story of Deanna Carpenter, a friend of mine who used to be a successful sales rep at a local title company. Her hobby was doing custom flower arrangements for people. She started out buying dried flowers at market, and then she needed more, and soon the garage wasn't big enough. Increasingly unhappy at her work, she decided to rent a small retail office space near her home and work parttime doing custom orders. Her bosses were unhappy about cutting her hours, but she gave them no choice. Soon, she needed even more space. She turned in her letter of resignation and began pouring her full energies and heart into her flowering.

Yesterday I went to see her newest place. She has an entire building now, where she sells not only flower arrangements but also antiques, artwork, candles, old books, and all the things she loves to collect herself. Every Friday evening she has a wine and cheese party to benefit a local charity.

In the midst of all this the competitor of her former title company offered her a job at nearly twice the substantial salary she had been making. Stuck in the middle of a start-up cash crunch, she was sorely tempted to take the job. But after really searching her heart, she turned them down. She now has hired an extra person to help handle the customers, has a website, and has expanded into another retail outlet in New Mexico. I asked her if everything was going according to plan.

She looked around her store with obvious delight and laughed, "I never had a plan. But I am living my vision."

This, to me, is the essence of success. Living your vision. It is also the essence of being a spiritreneur. In order to succeed as a spiritreneur the only way to do it is this: throw your heart over the bar, and your body will follow. After you've completed your first jump, pick your heart up, dust it off, walk around a bit to get the lay of the land, and then throw your heart over the next bar, knowing that it will be higher than the last.

Jesus did not live each day according to a written plan. But his vision did shape each day's activities—what he would do, what he would not do. Only in retrospect could it resemble a formalized business plan.

As I said earlier—I am all for business plans. I collect them. I also collect briefcases and organizers. But I have no illusion that plans make for success. It is only people, passionately following their visions, that make things successful.

Perhaps we are killing too many trees and not spending enough time on our knees. Perhaps we should stop saying thank you and please and instead go follow the birds and the bees . . . who dance and soar, never the same way twice, yet always find their way home.

Jesus knew a business plan would not save him.

Questions

1. Are you counting on a business plan to be a substitute for your vision?
2. How many pages would it take to describe your vision?

3. How clear is it?
4. How real is it?
5. What would you give to accomplish it?
6. What is the difference between a business plan and a vision?
7. Why do people sometimes confuse the two, and what are the ramifications of that?

Dear Lord,

Help me realize that we are accounted righteous by our faith, not by our works, lest any of us should boast. Help me get more into the dance of life, and less into the details.

Amen

HE PREPARED FOR DÉJÀ VU
ALL OVER AGAIN

How many times must you forgive? Seventy times seven . . .

—Matthew 18:22

Sister Ruth Marlene Fox shares in *The Living Word Devotional* that a friend revealed to her that when she began watching football games on television, she was initially unfamiliar with the "instant replay" feature. She turned to the person sitting beside her and asked, "Why do they keep making the same mistakes over and over?"

Jesus was well prepared for the instant replay or "déjà vu all over again" (as Yogi Berra once termed it). Jesus had to forgive Peter not once but three times before Peter's courage kicked in. When his disciples fled in fear at the Crucifixion, Jesus knew their fears, once again, had overcome their faith. Nevertheless, he didn't give up on them.

Your business will reflect both your highest ideals and your deepest issues. Therefore it should come as no surprise when you look up and think, "Haven't we been around this mountain before?" I am reminded of a verse in Ecclesiastes that reads:

Southward goes
the wind, then
turns to the north;
it turns and
turns again;
then back to its
circling goes
the wind.
(Ecclesiastes 1:6)

Some issues and problems just seem to keep coming around again.

I talked with a CEO who has had an 80 percent turnover in one of his divisions. That division is run by his wife. One can only wonder what issues—perhaps inherited—she is struggling with. Perhaps she could benefit from some counseling to gain insight into her soul. Or she will keep hiring and firing, always blaming others for the problems in the division.

Recently a young businessman shared with me that he is amazed at how often he keeps running into the same issues in his work—with only the names and the faces changed. "Could it be reflecting something that is unresolved in me?" he asked. I nodded and later shared my story.

For the last fifteen years I have fluctuated between a desire for expansion and a desire for the freedom of a simple life. My friend and mentor Catherine has watched this process with the unique blend of fascination and frustration that friendship often brings. She knows, for example, that every three years I will ramp up—and hire an aggressive marketing director. And she knows, and has accurately predicted, the ultimate disillusionment, distraction, and downsizing that always seems to follow. Every time I'm doing it—expanding or contracting—I am absolutely convinced I am doing the right thing.

The truth is, I can't find a good director of marketing because deep down in my bones I'm not sure I want to be marketed. Catherine's theory is that my soul is the battlefield where the desires of my father to succeed are at war with his other desire, which was to be free.

My father turned down multiple promotions in his company so he could keep the family in one place. He once turned down a Kentucky Fried Chicken franchise because he said he didn't think children should have to fry chickens after school, which he knew we would have had to do. I remember the day he got elected president of the neighborhood parks association as being one of the proudest days of my life. We kids worked many weekends with him clearing away tumbleweeds from tennis courts and painting the tool shed by the pool and expanding the zone of membership to include some of the poorer houses "outside the green." The saddest thing of all is that I don't think my father ever really saw himself as successful. His older brother was a war hero. Dad never went overseas. Uncle Joe worked at the Pentagon. Dad sold coffee for a living.

And that feeling—of never having climbed to the top of the highest mountain—haunted him even as he dodged it, ran around it, outmaneuvered it all his life.

I think that's why he would ask me, "What have you done lately?" even as he grabbed his tennis racket and headed out the door.

And so I sit ready to hire yet another marketing director, with a brand-new expansion plan spread out before me. Perhaps two years and 364 days from now I will say, "Catherine, I've been thinking. It's time to simplify." And she'll smile and say to herself, "Déjà vu all over again."

She is patient with me, as you must be with yourself when you can't seem to get it right the first time . . . When the same issues and questions and conflicts keep appearing in different costumes, wearing different names. These are the times when it's good to look into your soul. It can't always be *them* who's wrong. You know that. So do they.

Lord, how many times is it going to take me to get it right? Five? Six? Seven?

Maybe seventy times seven.

That is the number that comes to mind when I think of "déjà vu."

Jesus prepared for déjà vu all over again.

Questions

1. Do you keep running into the same issues in your life—only with different names and dates attached?
2. If so, how much time have you spent looking within yourself, rather than flipping through new résumés for the answer?
3. What issues did your parents have that might have been passed on to you?

Dear Lord,
I think I've seen this rock before. It seems I've been traveling in circles for days. Lord, please lift me to the mountain where I can finally get a clearer view.
Amen

HE DEFLECTED SPEARS AND ARROWS

The chief priests and the teachers of the law were standing there, vehemently accusing him.

—Luke 23:10

The glorified images we have of Jesus—walking on water, feeding the five thousand, raising Lazarus from the dead—sometimes make it easy to overlook very hard days and challenges Jesus faced.

The fact that Jesus was born and then lived to the age of thirty to begin his ministries came about because of the faith and survival skills of his parents. Joseph could easily have divorced Mary when he learned that she was pregnant, but he did not, ensuring Jesus a solid, two-parent home. Joseph and Mary also narrowly escaped the bloodthirsty soldiers of King Herod, who ordered all male Jewish newborn children to be slain, lest the prophesied "king" rise up among them. So Jesus was no stranger to danger by the time he grew up—nor did he fear it.

Yet he was not brazenly careless, either, with his divine

powers. Scripture shows Jesus slipping away through a crowd early in his ministry to avoid capture.

His own family, at one point, wanted to have him "put away" in order to avoid further and future embarrassment to the family name. Again Jesus escaped (Mark 6:31, 3:7–9, 6:45, 7:24; Matthew 13:54–58).

Another time, after healing a young man, he told him to tell no one what had happened. Jesus was aware that his deeds would bring controversy and indeed he predicted as much, saying, "I have not come to bring peace, but a sword." It wasn't long into his ministry when the critics and his enemies began to try to trip him up in order to discredit him. If there had been tabloid rags at the time they might have been flush with the headlines such as:

Nazarene Claims to Be Son of God!
OR
Miracles Follow Carpenter!
OR
Religious Experts Agree: Jesus Is from the Devil!

How did Jesus survive these highly personal attacks? The jealousy and small-mindedness of his high school buddies and the church leaders of the village were perhaps inevitable for anyone who rises above the crowd to do noble things. My mother once advised me, "Honey, the secret of peace is never take insults personally, even if they are directed at you."

When I spoke to the Parliament of the British Virgin Islands, one of the complaints the representatives had concerned the mud throwing and arrows they had to endure and survive in order to get to a place of "service"! It's bizarre how we worship celebrities whose focus is often only on themselves, and savage people who are simply trying to serve us.

Spiritreneurs must be prepared for the spears and arrows that may be hurled at us once we get into the palace, because those who dare to achieve and step out really annoy those who would rather stay where they are. Goliath never got off a shot at the emboldened shepherd boy David, but King Saul, the king he "saved," hurled spears and arrows at him multiple times.

Joseph had to survive the jealous wiles of his brothers, and so it continues today—the bitter rivalries among those of us called to be "family."

So, given that we will be wearing "target" T-shirts as soon as we achieve some modicum of success, how do we prepare ourselves?

Here are a few practical spear-dodging tips that might help you.

1. *Tighten up your relationship with God.* Saturate yourself with God's words of power and comfort, as David did when he was hiding out in the hills, as Jesus did in his final night in the Garden. This is ultimately the only relationship that matters, so make sure it is solid.

2. *Consider the source.* Jesus knew what motivated his enemies, and he said so. They had no interest in his well-being. He kept that in mind at all times.

3. *Turn their questions back on them.* Jesus was a master at getting to the heart of people by using the swords aimed at him

to reveal others' hearts. "Are you the King of the Jews?" demanded one. And he replied, "Who do you think I am?" (Luke 22:66). "Isn't it against the law to heal on the Sabbath?" asked another. "If your neighbor's sheep fell into a ditch on the Sabbath, would you get it out?" he replied (Matthew 12:10–11).

4. *Realize you don't have to respond to every insult.* "And they spat on him saying, 'Prophesy to us. Who hit you?' And to this he answered not a word" (Matthew 26:68).

5. *Tell the truth.* Jesus spoke the truth as he saw it, knowing that the truth would always set people free. When you tell the truth, you have nothing to fear.

6. *Keep your eye on God's prize, not theirs.* Remember, there is only one heart that you are responsible for pleasing, and it does not beat in any human breast.

The more Jesus grew in influence and power, the more he became a target. He very wisely learned to deflect the spears and arrows. Proverbs 19:11 reads, "A wise man restrains his anger and overlooks insults."

Perhaps Paul said it best when he warned us to "use every piece of God's armor to resist the enemy when he attacks, and when it is all over, you will be standing up. But to do this you will need the strong belt of truth and the breastplate of God's approval. Wear shoes that are able to speed you on as you preach the Good News of peace with God. In every battle you will need the helmet of salvation and the sword of the Spirit, which is the Word of God" (Ephesians 6:13–17, The Living Bible).

Jesus deflected spears and arrows.

Questions

1. What spears and arrows are being hurled at you?
2. By whom?
3. What does God say about it?
4. How are you responding?

Dear Lord,
You were a master at not getting thrown off course by the
slings and arrows of your enemies. Help me know and do
only your will, and take all comfort from that.

Amen

HE KNEW WHERE THE BULL WAS

Thou shalt have no other gods before me.
—Deuteronomy 5:7–8

I suspect that each of us has a bull in our closet . . . the bull that we melt all our energies into and then worship and serve. We are a society of bull worshippers—the headlines shout it out every day. For some of us the bull is power, for some of us it is fame—fortune—financial success—beauty—sex—acceptance—"being liked."

Our bulls not only sleep in our closets, they snort and stomp in our calendars, demanding to be put at the top of our priority lists. No matter how much we feed them, they always want more.

A ten-year-old once wrote in his Sunday School class essay: "The reason the Israelites made a golden calf in the desert is because they didn't have enough gold to make a bull."

As spiritreneurs we must learn to recognize—and control—our own "bull." Are we, through daily activities, honoring God or just feeding the beast?

"And he found *in the temple* those who sold oxen and sheep and doves, and the money changers doing business. When he had made a whip of cords, he drove them all out of the temple . . . And he said to those who sold the doves 'Take these things away. Do not make my Father's house a house of merchandise!' " (John 2:13–15).

Jesus put the bull in its place when he angrily overturned the money changers' tables in the temple. He was demanding that business respect and revere the sacred.

I had an interesting dream not too long ago which awakened me to the dangers of "uncontrolled bull."

In the dream I was entertaining all of my former bridesmaids. We were picnicking out on the lawn behind a beautiful Victorian farmhouse. Two of the bridesmaids, Linda and Deb, had their five-year-old niece and daughter, Melissa and Ashley, with them. We were all clothed in white comfortable cotton dresses, and after a picnic of strawberries and some other lavishly prepared hors d'oeuvres, they all decided to lie down for a nap on a huge white comforter. As everyone settled in to this idyllic scene I decided to take a walk down the road.

I'd gone about a hundred yards when I noticed that someone had let my prize bull into the pasture where the farmhouse was. I began to run and scream, "No!" In horror I watched as the bull took off in a fury, straight toward my sleeping guests. When I finally arrived the damage had been done. The two children were trembling and covered in blood. As I tried to find a place on their faces that wasn't bleeding I awakened, crying, "How did this happen? How could I have let this happen?"

That dream stayed with me for weeks—and is with me still. I looked up all the symbols in my dream-analysis books, prayed about it, and talked it over with friends. To me Melissa and Ashley represent childhood innocence and wonder. The farmhouse scene with the bridesmaids represents a sense of joy and comfort at just being with family and friends. The bull represents my inner ambition and drive to succeed, to reproduce, multiply, and dominate—in other words, the "business" side of me. I realized from the dream that I could not and should not let the bull of business destroy my friendships, or my own childhood sense of wonder and possibility. I should keep the bull in its place, and not let it dominate my life.

1. God has nothing against wealth. He made Solomon the richest man in the world.

2. God has nothing against fame. In Kings, He promised to make King David's name and fame endure to all generations.

Bulls and other business activities are fine, as long as we don't make them our gods, as long as we don't let them make a mess of our soul—which wants to bask in the sunshine of God's love.

Right after that dream I called Linda and flew to Portland to see her. I also brought her a framed picture of Melissa I had taken, with the five-year-old standing in her blue denim dress, smilingly lifting a rose to her lips. There was a wisp of red hair across her face, and she stood in a pose that was part ballerina, part princess, all wrapped in innocence. We did not talk about business the whole time I was there. I am learning to recognize my bull—and keep it in the pen where it belongs, lest it trample my soul.

Jesus knew where the bull was.

Questions

1. What golden calf are you worshipping? Be honest.
2. How do you feed it, and how often?
3. Why is it important to recognize your own personal "bull"?
4. Do you have an unpenned bull that is in danger of destroying your relationship with God? With others? With yourself?
5. How are you going to keep the bull in its place?

Dear Lord,
You were great at detecting bulls masquerading as priests:
Give me your discerning power. Turn your lamp upon my
heart. Clean out my closets and my pastures and come sit
with me on a white comforter, safe in the afternoon sun,
knowing you—and time with you—is all I truly desire.
                                        Amen

HE HAD X-RAY VISION

Jesus was able to see into the hearts of all people.

—Mark 2:8

Superman was able to perform heroic wonders due in no small part to his extraordinary gifts. One of my favorites of the gifts he had was X-ray vision. With it he was able to discern exactly where the bomb was located or where Jimmy Olsen was being held hostage. No wall was so thick that Superman's X-ray vision couldn't penetrate it—usually just in time.

One of the gifts that the Holy Spirit bestows is the gift of discernment. According to *Webster's Dictionary*, discernment means: "the faculty of showing good judgment and under-standing; discrimination; acuteness of judgment and under-standing." To me, the word *discernment* is another description for spiritual X-ray vision. Jesus had X-ray Vision.

This ability allowed him to see through the flattering words and insincere intentions that surrounded him as he went about his mission. Discernment is the ability to get to the heart of things—quickly—without getting distracted by the obstacles and detour signs that clutter the road.

I know a few people who have that gift of discernment. My mother is one of them. Catherine is another.

Yet for those who don't feel naturally gifted with X-ray vision of the heart, here is a simple formula that most two-year-olds innately understand. It is the persistent and pervasive use of the word *why.*

I believe that most of us function several levels above the real "why" in our lives. Being able to get to the foundational "why" in your life can save you immeasurable time, tears, and money.

For example, not too long ago I met an ambitious and successful music executive who seemed 100 percent into his job. The solid black outfit, the slicked-back hair, the ever-present pager and cellular phone seemed to shout that this was a man on the fast track to bigger and better things. In fact, our entire first conversation consisted of his plans for the company label, and he probed me with questions that were designed to see where my organization's plan might serve his. I was familiar with this type of intensity, so I just went along, answering each question he asked. After he heard me speak he invited me to dinner, and then proceeded to pour out his life's story—an incredible tale of abuse and redemption that included his efforts to support a family abandoned by an abusive father.

At this point I began to ask him questions about his future plans. He said he planned to sign three new artists to his company's record label and had been working on the deals for some time. I then asked him the first why: "Why are these deals important to you?" He paused, then said, "Because these deals would almost ensure me a promotion." Second why: "Why is a promotion important to you?" His answer— "Because then they would pay me a lot more money." Third why: "Why is making a lot more money important to you?"

He grew very quiet and then said in a whisper, "Because then I could afford to record my own songs." Bingo. Three whys down and we were into his true motivating force. He was trapped in a parallel career—one that is close to what he wanted to do, but not right on it. He was promoting other recording artists when what he really wanted to be was a recording artist himself. I invited him to one of our Path training seminars to help him clarify his mission. He has since actively been preparing demo songs of his material.

Jesus was a master at asking questions. He knew that people who answered honestly wanted the truth, while people who tried to multiply confusion with vague or meaningless answers didn't want truth, they just wanted attention. He had little time or patience with these.

What a gift to have X-ray vision! To be able to get to the heart of the issue. Many of our activities in business stem from unclear intentions or unmet personality needs. What are we really trying to accomplish, and why? You can use it to help save your friends. It rarely works on yourself, I've found, so find people who can use the whys with you, and you should be in very good hands.

"You shall know the truth and the truth shall set you free" (John 8:32).

Jesus had X-ray vision.

Questions

1. Do you agree that most of us live several levels above the real why? If so, give examples.
2. Is that true in your life?
3. Why is the "why" more important to know than the "who, when, where, and how"?
4. Can you use this tool in multiple areas of decision making? Name five.

Dear Lord,
Please give me the gift of discernment so that I can see into the hearts of others—not for my own purposes, but so that I too can help set them free.
                    Amen

HE DID NOT FEAR
THREATENING LETTERS

He said you have no power over me . . .
—John 19:11

I work hard to maintain my credit rating, so when I received notice that my mortgage payment was thirty days late, I promptly got on the phone. In the midst of refinancing my Texas and New Mexico property, it seems some confusion had occurred regarding the two deeds. My automatic draft had been canceled so I could personally deliver a check, but then the documents didn't show up in time so I was notified not to make any payment. Subsequently I received a redlined letter stating I was in danger of losing my property due to the missing payment. I was given a list of credit counselors to call. This upset me, so I called the woman who was coordinating the refinance and told her that I had received threatening correspondence regarding my property and credit standing.

Debbie, who sounded on the phone as if she were about twenty years old, paused a moment and then said in her most dramatic voice, "Oooh—a threatening letter!"

I was so taken aback by her humorous perspective that I burst out laughing. This serious letter, which at the time was blocking the entire horizon line of my future, was seen by this Generation Xer for what it truly was—an oversight, a hiccup, a gnat on the timeline of life.

It made me think of how spiritreneurs regularly face threatening letters of some sort—either written out in tangible form or spelled out word for word at night while we lie sleeping, or trying to sleep.

Nehemiah received a threatening letter as he was rebuilding the walls of Jerusalem.

"We hear you are actually leading a rebellion against the king. He's heard it too and he wants you to come down from there."

To which Nehemiah replied, "I am doing a great work and I cannot come down" (Nehemiah 6:3).

David's brothers tried to keep him from fighting Goliath. Joseph's brothers tried to keep him from rising to power over them. Jesus received several warnings about ceasing and desisting from his work.

In fact, if you haven't received a threatening letter in your mind or otherwise, warning you of imminent danger to your life and very soul if you continue on this path, you probably are sitting in a rocking chair, eyes permanently affixed to the "comfort zone."

I have a friend who decided to launch a conference, inviting business leaders from around the world to convene and discuss the spiritual aspects of their work. Initially her pastor was supportive, and he even offered to speak at the event. That is until it looked as though it was going to be really successful. Suddenly, this pastor realized that her event was going to outshine all the ones he had put on.

So, the night before the conference was to begin, he wrote her a letter and hand-delivered it. As she unfolded it and read it before him she couldn't believe the words on the page.

> *My Dear Sister—*
> *After much prayer and fasting, I and the Church Board have decided that this event is not from God—but from the devil himself. Therefore you are to call all guests and participants immediately, and turn over the mailing list to our church so we may pray over the souls who were about to be duped by Satan working through you.*

Barbara looked at him and said, "I am doing a great work, Pastor Brown, and I cannot and will not end it now." With that, she invited him to leave.

Oooh—a threatening letter! Now she knew it was going to succeed—and it did, beyond her wildest imaginings. The conference that she and her mother ended up bankrolling after the church pulled out has now become an annual event, attended by business leaders and supported by foundations from around the world. A threatening letter did not stop her great work.

Eleanor Roosevelt was a vigorous campaigner for civil rights. It is said that she received a letter threatening her life if she showed up to speak at a civil rights rally in a small town in Mississippi. The city officials who received the letter sent an accompanying note urging her to stay away because they could not guarantee her safety. She wrote back stating that they were not responsible for her safety, and she and a friend drove their own car into the city (with a loaded pistol sitting between them). She spoke at the rally, urging a return to common decency, showing uncommon courage in the face of hatred and fear.

"With the Lord on my side, I fear nothing" (Hebrews 13:6).

The young Nazarene was warned frequently about the dangerous consequences of his mission.

Jesus did not fear threatening letters.

Questions

1. What threatening letters have you received, or could you receive, if you launch the venture God is calling you toward?
2. How will you respond?
3. What are you made of—really?

Dear Lord,
Make it so the only letter I know is the one you've written to me, the one that says that I can do all things—if only I believe. Let me now not draw back in fear the first time a shadow falls across my path, but rather let me press on to receive the crown you've inscribed—and are saving for me—who shall in all ways, through you, be victorious.

Amen

HE OVERCAME THE DESPERADOES

He gave them power over unclean spirits.
—Mark 6:7

Nothing attracts the hungry like the whiff of success. Once your visibility rises, so do poor relatives—or should I say—wannabe relatives. Jesus attracted the largest crowds when he did his miracles and gave out sandwiches besides. Looking out over the crowds he harbored no illusions about what they really wanted from him—power—not prophecy. He knew that the human heart can be easily swayed by trivial, day-to-day needs and wants, and so he put his trust only in God.

As someone who loves to help people plan their lives, I attract a lot of people with unplanned lives. Nothing wrong with that, except that some people's lives are in transition, not in the natural ebb and flow of life but due to some undercurrent of need and desperation.

One principle that has been painfully learned in our organization is to keep the social work mentality out of the hiring process. The other principle we've learned is that if someone is beating down your door to be a part of your organization, it's often the pantry, not the principles, that they are after.

Sandra Steen, a woman named Entrepreneur of the Year, and I found ourselves in the same steam room after our mutual presentations in the Bahamas.

As we were sitting there discussing our mutual journeys, I told her about *Jesus, Inc.* I said, "I'm writing a chapter called 'He Overcame the Desperadoes.' Do you think that has a place in a book about spiritreneurship?"

"Laurie," she said, wiping the steam from her face, "that should be one of the first chapters!" She then shared with me how one of her most difficult lessons was identifying people whose sole intent was not to help you, but do you harm.

Unfortunately, not everyone who would do you damage wears a black cape and a thin mustache, accompanied by a sound-track of hisses, boos, or eerie music. The people who have caused me the most stress have all been well-dressed, sociable, charming individuals who rolled out a red carpet of flattery and promises. Their stated intent was to help me reach my goals but their actual intent was to try to get the gold.

I feel no shame in sharing these examples because even Jesus hired Judas. Whether Jesus knew Judas was a desper-ado when he hired him or whether he only realized it toward the end is a cause for endless debate and theological specula-tion. All I know is that if Jesus wasn't able to escape without a bad apple on his team, I don't know why we think we can.

I once signed a personal note for a debt that was not fully mine. I'm still paying that one off.

I don't beat myself up over these errors in judgment. Wisdom comes from experience—and experience is just a fancy name for failure.

In retrospect all of my bad deals or bad apples had a few common characteristics. One was, they all had dollar signs in their eyes. Business author and consultant Ken Blanchard says that Dr. Norman Vincent Peale once told him, "If one of the first things people tell you is how much money they're going to make for you, walk away. The best partnerships are based on shared goals and values, not formulas for splitting the loot."

Another thing these "bad apples" had in common was a sense of urgency. Deals had to be signed right away or the "window of opportunity" would disappear. God's windows don't have frames around them—and they don't disappear.

A spiritreneur I know from Canada, who helped turn his grandfather and father's business into a multibillion-dollar enterprise, said his grandfather once told him that "no business ever suffered from moving slowly, if it is headed in the right direction."

Another trait of the deperadoes is that it is difficult to get straight and simple answers from them. Trying to get specifics out of them is like trying to nail down Jell-O. The only thing they ever want to sign is your checks, yet their promised goods are never really visible or deliverable—for a host of excuses or reasons.

Jesus said, "Let your yes be yes and your no be no" (Matthew 5:37). A multiplication of words often indicates a jumbled brain.

I am in awe of the courage and trust of Jesus, turning over the use of his name and the keys to the kingdom to a ragtag bunch of his friends. But to him they were the beloved, and all of them—with the exception of one—ultimately came through. Jesus refused to let one bad apple spoil the whole barrel.

"And while he was still speaking, Judas came, one of the twelve, and he kissed him. Then they came up and laid hands on Jesus and seized him." Yet later Jesus said, "Father, forgive them for they know not what they do . . ." And after his death the angel said, "He is not here, for he has risen, just like he said" (Matthew 26:47–50, Luke 23:34, Matthew 28:6).

Jesus overcame the desperadoes.

Questions

1. What are some characteristics or clues that might alert you to a "desperado"?
2. What steps have you taken to ensure that your team is a loyal and sincere one?
3. Would you agree that parents and close friends might be a valuable screening tool, though we often discount their advice or subconsciously rebel against it?
4. What possible clues might Jesus have seen that Judas's heart was not truly with him?

Dear Lord,
Help me avoid the desperadoes. Help me search my own heart and my intentions so I will not offer them an easy mark. Every biblical hero had their challenges and betrayers and still managed to emerge triumphant in you. Let the same be said of me, O Lord. Let the same be said of me.
Amen

HE DIDN'T LET THE WINDS DRIVE HIM CRAZY

And as they got into the boat, the wind ceased.
—Matthew 14:32

Those of us who live in West Texas are accustomed to the high desert winds that come sweeping through the region every spring.

Therefore I had an understanding when I read case histories of pioneer women on the Great Plains who literally went mad because of the winds. They had no mountains to shelter or surround them. One woman wrote in her journal about the wind's incessant howling—through the cracks in the floor and the gap underneath the door. Sometimes, she wrote, all she could hear was the shrieking and howling of a force not of her own making. Eventually she ran out of the house screaming and was never heard from again.

I understand why David wrote in Psalms that the Lord was like a sheltering rock . . . that the Lord surrounded his people with love like the mountains surround Jerusalem (Psalms

94:22, Psalms 125:2). He also wrote "Happy are those who take refuge in the Lord" (Psalms 34:9).

Wind represents the forces and pressures and demands not of our own making. Spiritreneurs must work hard to create a quiet place—a place free from the wind. We must find a boat we can climb into, and also pray that the wind may cease.

Imagine Peter's relief when the Lord reached out and took his hand, just as he was about to go under. Peter had walked on water as far as he could on his own, and that's when he cried out for the Lord's help. The Lord reached out and took his hand, and immediately when he and Jesus got into the boat, the wind ceased.

Keeping—and finding—your quiet place within is a task worthy of great focus. Consider the results of a study conducted by Pitney Bowes, quoted in *American Demographics* magazine:

> *The average office denizen fields more than 200*
> *outgoing and incoming messages a day: 52 telephone calls,*
> *36 e-mail messages, 23 voice-mail messages,*
> *18 postal mail, 18 interoffice mail, 14 faxes, 13 Post-it notes,*
> *9 telephone message slips, 8 pager messages,*
> *4 cellular phone calls, 4 overnight courier/messengers,*
> *and 3 overnight mail.*

Keeping your balance means maintaining supreme focus— especially in high winds.

Finding a balance means going to a sheltering place. Every spiritreneur absolutely must have—and guard—a sheltering place, even if it is only twenty minutes in the bathtub. Mothers with children, businessmen with a demanding board of directors, fathers with children, women with a demanding itinerary are all too easily accessible now with cell phones, pagers, e-mail, and all the other "conveniences" that let us get in touch with one another. Jesus was highly visible, but he also knew how to disappear.

According to Dr. Joyce Brothers, the favorite tool of a procrastinator is a "To Do" list. The favorite tool of a spiritreneur must be a "Not Done" list. I shock myself even as I write this. Could God want us to have and maintain a Not Done list? Jesus said as much when he praised Mary for dropping her dish towel to come commune with him while Martha was busy in the kitchen, clicking off her To Do list. To soften the blow of the very idea of having a Not Done list, perhaps we should call the list a "Not Done by Me" list.

Spiritreneurs must learn to delegate in order that they can go to a quiet place. This isn't easy, considering that new research from Media Metrix shows that more than half of computer-owning households have a television in the same room as their computer. Of those households, 95 percent say the TV and computer are on simultaneously some or most of the time.

I am constantly amazed at professional women friends I have who still clean their own houses, and then complain about being exhausted. One friend I have boldly declared that she was going to take an art class on Tuesday nights, no matter what, and her husband easily agreed to watch the two boys while she did so. She had found a way not to let the wind drive her crazy. Her husband helped create a sheltering place for her. After a few classes, she found herself wondering why it had taken her ten years to get up the courage—the focus—to say, "I need this time for me."

*The Lord is my shepherd; I shall not want. He maketh me to
lie down in green pastures; he leadeth me beside the still
waters. He restoreth my soul. He leadeth me in the paths of
righteousness for his name's sake. Yea, though I walk
through the valley of the shadow of death, I will fear no evil;
for thou art with me; thy rod and thy staff they comfort me.
Thou preparest a table before me in the presence of mine
enemies; thou anointest my head with oil; my cup runneth
over. Surely goodness and mercy shall follow me all the days
of my life; and I will dwell in the house of the Lord forever.*
(Psalm 23)

*Yahweh is my rock
and my fortress,
My deliverer is my God.
I take my refuge in him.
My rock,
My shield,
My saving strength,
my stronghold,
my place of refuge.*
(2 Samuel 22:2–3)

Jesus didn't let the winds drive him crazy.

Questions

1. Where and what is your sheltering place?
2. How fiercely do you guard it? How?

3. What howling winds are about to drive you shrieking from the hut?
4. Make out a list right now of things that will no longer be done by you.
5. Do so with love and firmness and then share it with those who can help become your sheltering place.

Dear Lord,
You went often alone to pray to get out of the winds of pre-vailing opinion and popularity and lust for power. Help me find and create a sheltering place, where only You are welcome—as my companion—my friend.

Amen

THE LESSONS: LEARNING THROUGH THE WISDOM AND MISTAKES OF OTHERS

Things have now calmed down. You're no longer subjected to the roller-coaster ride that marks the beginning of any new enterprise. Yet somehow you have entered the zone of "one step forward, two steps back." You may feel at times as if you are wandering in circles, not getting anywhere at all. "Haven't I seen that rock before?" is a common refrain as lessons on leadership, discipline, persistence, and discernment are learned one by one.

What stretches out before you is a seeming desert plain. Gone are the familiar pyramids of your former captivity. Faded also are the shouts of fear and glory you experienced at the last minute of your "Lurch." The sea parted and you walked through unharmed.

Now all you have is "quail, quail, quail, manna, manna, manna." God is providing for you, sure, but where are the great revelations? The explosive growth? Your en-

emies are no longer strangers. The enemies that now haunt you are those inside. Their names are Boredom, Monotony, Politics, Trivialities. This is the time for the daily lessons—where battles are won in little ways.

God told the Israelites that they would not conquer the Promised Land all at once, lest it prove too much for them. And so you move forward slowly, learning as you go. You sit around the campfire and lean forward to hear the elders—knowing there are still dangers ahead mixed in with the promises. For tonight, at least, the wolves seem very far away. It is here in the Lessons, that we learn to "sweat the small stuff," and in so doing, win big.

HE DID EVERYTHING AUTL

Whatever your work is, put your whole heart into it as if it were for the Lord.

—Colossians 3:23

Jesus did everything AUTL. As Unto the Lord. When he made a chair he wasn't making it for Joseph, really. He was making it for the Lord. If every single person in business could have and practice this philosophy, imagine what kind of customer service we would have in this country. One of the surest signs of spirituality in business is excellence.

Ironically, I encounter people every day, many claiming to be Christians, who are so intent on doing heavenly things that they leave the worldly things undone. I recently counseled a young man who declares that his mission is to be a financial ambassador for the Kingdom of God. He is working on mega-million-dollar deals, he claims, yet recently lost his credit due to the inability to pay his own bills. One has to wonder about this man's credibility when it comes to financial matters. Doesn't he realize that how we handle small matters will determine how, and if, we handle great ones?

Do you think Jesus was a lousy carpenter? Are we not to handle every object, every transaction, every moment—as a gift from God? A better way to get through the day is to do it As Unto the Lord.

In the same breath I must argue that there are many ways to serve the Lord, and we shouldn't get stuck in ways that don't fit our highest gifts.

The niece of a friend of mine was sharing about the challenges she faces in a small rural town in a state we shall pretend is Mississippi. Ashley attends a small high school there in a town called Bend. There are twelve students in her graduating class. She was lamenting to me over a brunch that "this town is so backwards it named itself Bend—even though it is really an intersection. I guess Intersection was already taken."

"It is," piped in her cousin, reaching for a pickle.

"Go on," I urged Ashley, sensing a story about to unfold.

"Well, I am determined that I am not going to end up living in this town, married to someone who is probably a distantly related cousin. I study hard—real hard. The biggest thing in this town is football. It is so big, in fact, that a new teacher got suspended recently for assigning homework during football season! Anyway, every week we have a pep rally for the team. I find this a big waste of time, so I hide out in the girls' locker room, reading my college preparatory books. The coach found me in there one day and insisted that I go sit in the stands with the rest of the school. Reluctantly, I agreed. But since the pep rallies last three hours I took my books up into the stands with me."

Ashley sighed as she reached for another glass of punch. "The principal saw me up in the stands and cornered me after the pep rally. 'I need to see you in my office, young lady,' he shouted. I could tell he was really mad. I went to his office where I found him, the coach, and three of my other teachers. He started yelling the minute I walked in. 'Ashley, You are either *for* Bend, or *against* Bend! Which shall it be?' "

By this time I was laughing so hard I thought I was going to choke on my carrot. I could see it so clearly—the small-minded, intense principal trying to intimidate a bright, college-bound girl whose priorities seemed so misplaced.

I really find ultimatums like that a sign of small-mindedness. And I see it so often in Christianity. Evangelicals line up against Catholics against Baptists against Methodists against all others and shout, "You are either *for* God, or you are *against* God! Which shall it be?"

Is a student studying in the stands *against* the school she attends because she does not particularly care to jump up and down with its mascot? Can't she honor the school, and make its teachers and principals proud, by maybe someday coming up with a cure for cancer? By doing something that has nothing to do with the prevailing rah-rah pastime?

Are monks for God, or against God? Are auto mechanics for God, or against God? It all depends. If a monk joins a monastery to hide from the world, is he truly honoring God, or looking for a way to escape relationships? If an auto mechanic does his work As Unto the Lord, is he for God, or against God? The heart, and the work, will always tell.

God doesn't care what particular job you do. God doesn't care whether you are up in the stands studying or down on the field, playing your heart out. The question is, are you doing what you're doing As Unto the Lord?

Jesus did his work AUTL.

Questions

1. Can you think of an example where you recently did your work AUTL?
2. When you didn't do your work AUTL?
3. What were the results—in you, in your customers?
4. Can people serve God in ways that might not agree with yours?
5. Why could the AUTL principle transform business as we know it?
6. How much more can you do your work AUTL?

Dear Lord,
I work for only You. Please help me remember that, and do
everything as unto You.
Amen

HE SPENT TIME IN EGYPT

I have called my son out of Egypt.
—Matthew 2:15

Egypt in the Old Testament symbolizes a place of hardship for the Jews. For them it represented a land of harsh rulers and alien gods, and they left it as soon (and as often) as they could. I've been told that in Hebrew, Egypt also means "a narrow place, or a place of bondage."

Yet several of the Bible's most successful spiritreneurs spent a great deal of time there. Moses was raised in Pharaoh's court, and Joseph spent years of slavery and hard times in prison before he rose to become number one on Pharaoh's hit parade. For whatever reason, Egypt was a formative force in the lives of God's spiritreneurs. Jesus also spent time there, although we are uncertain as to how long.

We are told of the prophecy in Matthew 2:15: "Out of Egypt I have called my son." I believe Egypt is not only a place but also a metaphor for being where one doesn't want to be.

As we each evaluate our own history there may be a lot of Egypt in our past. An unhappy marriage, perhaps. A previous business failure. A work environment where we were made to feel put down and devalued.

Yet the joyous cry of every Christian is ultimate freedom, and freedom from "living in Egypt" is a right I believe belongs to all spiritreneurs.

Famed retail store designer J'Amy Owens, president of the Retail Group, worked for several years in an architectural firm as a sales representative. When her sales commissions outpaced the salaries of the principals themselves, they fired her. Only after she left did she realize how confined she had been. Teaming up with another architect who valued her visionary skills, she started a company that specializes in dramatic redesign of retail shops so shoppers have a more welcoming and stimulating experience. Her time at a drab, dull, architecture firm—Egypt—forged in her soul a passion for freedom in design which has made her legendary. All of us have to come from somewhere, and an unhappy place is just as good as any other place to "be from."

In the film *Music of the Heart* the mother of the woman played by Meryl Streep encourages Meryl to thank her ex-husband for leaving her. "Why should I thank him?" she asks as she straightens her ball gown on the way to performing a concert in Carnegie Hall. Her mother answers, "Because if he hadn't left you, none of this good would have happened."

Steve Jobs was exiled from his own company, Apple Computer, for several years. And what a difference it made. He returned with fresh ideas that repositioned the company in a new and powerful way.

Jesus spent formative time in Egypt, and it only made him better prepared for his mission. So, on your way out of town, kiss that Sphinx on the nose. God used it to teach you something you will soon need to know.

Jesus spent time in Egypt.

Questions

1. Have you spent time in Egypt? Are you there now? Describe what it was (is) like.
2. What formation might be taking place as a result of your having been there?
3. Why might God have put Egypt as well as Canaan on your spiritual map?

Dear Lord,
I'm ready to leave Egypt now. Thank you for the lessons.
                                                              Amen

HE DIDN'T LET THE FISH
SWALLOW HIM

The boy mastered the fish and pulled it onto the bank.
—Tobit 7:4, The Jerusalem Bible

One of my favorite stories in the Jerusalem Bible is that of Tobit and Raguel. An angel in disguise is sent to guard young Raguel on his journey. The angel assures Raguel's anxious father that "all will be well." The father believes that Raguel will be given God's red carpet treatment. Yet at their first stop on the first night of the trip, danger occurs. That first evening the boy and the disguised angel camped beside the Tigris River. The boy had gone down to the river to wash his feet when a great fish leapt out of the water and tried to swallow his foot. The boy gave a shout and the angel said, "Catch the fish, and do not let it go." After the boy pulled the fish onto the bank the angel said, "Cut it open; take out the gall, heart, and liver and set them aside because they have curative properties" (Tobit 10:2–5, The Jerusalem Bible). Later, the ground fish powder becomes the medicine that cures Raguel's bride-to-be and father-in-law.

I love this story because it reminds me that even though we have guardian angels we are not going to live a challenge-free existence. Every spiritreneur who sets out on a journey, assured in body and soul of God's good oversight and blessing, is still probably going to have to fight a few fish at some point down the line.

We would do well to realize that the problem that seems to have us in its grip is not as big as we are, not there by accident, and has hidden gifts within it we will later value as long as we master it and study its "innards."

Inc. magazine recently carried a story about a young entrepreneur who was determined to open up an online pet supply business. It was perhaps on his first night camping on the riverbank of his idea that a fish named reality grabbed him by the heel. It turns out that five much larger pet supply stores had beaten him to the concept. Undaunted even in the face of this seeming defeat, the young man found such a kinship with one of his competitors that they decided to help support him in a noncompetitive spin-off venture. Had he reacted with anger, indignation, or animosity against his "big fish" he might be pounding the pavement today. Instead, he thrives in an office they set up especially for him. The entrepreneur had set out on a journey toward success and did not let his supposed outcome become bigger than he was.

Jonah is a case of a spiritreneur who got so attached to his anticipated outcome that when God's plans changed, he didn't. Therefore, literally, the fish became bigger than he was and swallowed him up for three days. "Now the Lord had prepared a great fish to swallow Jonah. Jonah was in the belly of the fish for three days and three nights" (Jonah 1:17).

Jonah's supposed successful outcome was the destruction of Nineveh, which the Lord had prophesied through him. Yet somehow the people of Nineveh repented, thereby robbing Jonah of his supposed successful outcome. Jonah did not look at the situation and land his fish by saying, "With God, I can handle this unexpected event." Instead he pouted and brooded and quit—thus becoming fish food for a few days.

When Jesus was in the hands of the Roman soldiers, he knew even then that he was, through God's power, bigger than they were. This arrest and charade of a trial, culminating in a death sentence, would look to anyone like the ultimate defeat—a horrible wrong turn on the journey. Yet Jesus kept his perspective, knowing that his Crucifixion would contain the curative powers the world needed. He never conceded defeat, looking to God even with his last breath to make everything right again.

As a business owner I am well aware that my enterprise can at any moment turn and swallow me alive. I've seen it happen to many business people—haven't you? The journey that began in joy ends up engulfed in doubt and depression. I was shocked and saddened by the suicide of two of El Paso's prominent business leaders—one an insurance executive, the other a leader of one of the most successful job-retraining programs in the country. At some point, their problems swallowed them and consumed them. What a loss it was to all of us who knew and respected them.

Every spiritreneur I know wrestles daily with a fish trying to swallow his or her foot. How do I keep my balance here? How do I gain perspective? How do I pull this fish ashore and cook and eat it in triumph—before it swallows me?

Jesus kept his poise, his perspective, his power even with the jaws of a major problem locked on his very being.

He kept looking to God with confidence.

Jesus did not let the fish swallow him.

Questions

1. What problem has you by the foot right now?
2. Are you about to panic and let it pull you under?
3. When you wrestle it onto the shore, look to see what healing gift lies within its innards.
4. Remembering that you and God are bigger than any problem you face, why not enjoy the exercise of pulling it ashore?

Dear Lord,

You always seemed to enjoy fishing. Help me be like you, not Jonah, and pull my problem ashore so I can feast on its valuable lessons, and help heal others with its innards as well.

Amen

HE KNEW HE WAS "BIG ENOUGH"

A little one shall become a thousand, and a small one a strong nation. I, the Lord, will hasten it in its time.
—Isaiah 60:22

We live in a society that is obsessed with the size of things. How big is your house, your status, your bank account? How big is your company? One of the challenges every spiritreneur faces is: How big should I be? "Bigger is always better" seems to be the mantra in business.

Yet Jesus clearly valued quality, not quantity. He handpicked only a few disciples, when he could have had a cast of thousands. He traveled no more than thirty miles, displaying a desire to perform a series of meaningful acts at home, rather than conquer the world.

An often overlooked fact is that the huge Fortune 500 companies employ only 15 percent of America's workforce. The lions that really have the roar are the accumulated small businesses, which employ 85 percent of the workers in the United States. It is the quality of output of these small firms that determines the true strength of this nation.

Yet many small businesses owners yearn to get bigger, often to their detriment. They can grow to the point of losing control, sacrificing quality of life, sometimes breaking up families in the process. They fall prey to the sizzle and lose the steak.

A friend of mine recently lost her wedding and engagement ring. Her husband dilligently began a search for the perfect diamonds to replace it, studying the quality of each gem that the jeweler presented him. Finally her daughter cried in exasperation, "Mom, this is Texas! Doesn't he know that all we care about is size, not quality?"

I remember so clearly the pastor who wept with me because his congregation couldn't seem to grow beyond 120 members. When I asked him what the mission of the church was, he said, "To raise, grow, and nurture disciples."

"Well, if you turn out 120 well-raised disciples, you'd have ten times the number that Jesus had, and he changed the world!" I said, and then he looked up and smiled.

I personally admire the Quaker religion, which has an aversion to counting converts. One Quaker I spoke with told me, "We don't want numbers to be a source of pride—or a goal—of what we do. We are just here to serve the Lord, as best we can."

An evangelist boasted to me that their campaign had netted fifty thousand new converts. His group was planning more campaigns in other parts of the world. I then asked him if he knew what the number one problem facing the new churches was. He indicated he did not know. "Domestic violence," I said. "How many people are you devoting to that issue?" He turned and walked away. Numbers, not substance, is too often the goal.

The rise and fall of many dot-com companies reveals that at some point, quality and not just quantity has to kick in, even in the wild and wooly world of the new economy.

I learned the lesson of respecting small things when as a twelve-year-old I was assigned to a horse at camp that must have been a runt at birth. As I dejectedly watched all the older girls lead off their shining palominos and glorious sorrel quarterhorses, I thought to myself, "I'll never win any ribbons now."

The wrangler, Jake, must have read my mind. As he cinched up the saddle on my short, scrawny horse, he said, "Don't worry, kiddo. He ain't big, but he's big enough."

In fact, Big Enough was his name. When the final class started, it rained. Unfortunately I had forgotten to secure my yellow rain slicker on the back of the saddle. When Big Enough launched out of the gate to run the barrels, the slicker came loose and fanned out behind us like a huge yellow cape. I will never forget hanging on for dear life as Big Enough proceeded to twist, buck, turn, and squeal trying to unseat both me and the cape. I remembered that Jake had said, "The secret to staying on is to see you and your horse as one. Don't ever let daylight come between you and the saddle." I didn't, finally guiding him to a stop after a full two minutes of rodeo. At the end of the camp, to my delight and surprise, I received an award for outstanding horsemanship. When the camp owner handed out the award, he said, "She might not know how to tie on a rain slicker, but she sure knows how to stay on a horse."

I think about that story a lot for us spiritreneurs, because ultimately we will be judged not by the size of the horse we rode, but by how well we handled the horse we were assigned.

God does not care how big you are. He wants to know the size of your heart. If your business is a reflection of that, then you are a success.

In the Book of Revelation Jesus told the members of a small church, "I know that you are not very [big or] strong in numbers, but you have kept my commandments. Therefore they will recognize that I have loved you."

Jesus knew he was big enough.

Questions

1. Do you have feelings that you and your endeavor are not big enough?
2. If so, where do those feelings come from?
3. What do you think God would say to your feelings of "If only . . ."?
4. How can you combat the ego's need for constant comparisons?

Dear Lord,

When Jesus was born, he wasn't the biggest guy in town. Yet he was Big Enough. King David was a scrawny kid— the smallest among his brothers—but when he set out to toss rocks at a giant, he was Big Enough. The women who gathered at the cross and waited to carry your body home weren't very big women, but they were Big Enough. Help me, Lord, to look inside and ask only one question: Is my heart Big Enough for God? And let the answer be yes.

Amen

HE INVESTED HIS
EMOTIONS WISELY

Absalom's head got caught in the oak.
　　　　　　　　—2 Samuel 18:9

A bsalom was the most beautiful of David's sons. Scripture describes him as a man of great stature, with a head of hair so magnificent that he actually weighed it on occasion.

"Now in all Israel there was no one who was praised as much as Absalom for his good looks. From the sole of his foot to the crown of his head there was no blemish in him . . . He weighed the hair of his head at two hundred shekels according to the king's standard" (2 Samuel 14:25–26).

Absalom invested heavily in his hair—priding himself on his locks. He also invested heavily in self-aggrandizement, positioning himself outside the city gates to try to build a following of rebels who might help him overthrow his father's throne.

Absalom also invested heavily in revenge—slaying his half-brother for raping his sister Tamar. Absalom did not invest his emotions wisely. Absalom's ending is one of the most tragic and ironic twists of fate in Scripture. Running through some low-lying trees in an attempt to escape David's army, Absalom's big beautiful hair got stuck in an oak tree, pulling him off his mount. There he dangles helplessly while one of David's soldiers runs him through with his sword. Absalom literally dies hanging by one of his hang-ups.

Absalom, being David's son, was heir to a vast inheritance. Yet he squandered any chance he had of greatness by not investing wisely his most precious assets, which were his mind and emotions.

Most studies confirm that thoughts cause emotions, not vice versa, and Absalom's heavy investment in his physical appearance, his desire for revenge, his get-throne-quick schemes, all revealed a person who was not choosing wisely the directions of his thoughts. Thus, his emotions overcame him and led him to drastic acts (2 Samuel, chapters 13–18).

When I think of Jesus' recitation of the Seven Deadly Sins—all of them have to do with states of mind we can control. I've developed an acronym to help me remember the list more easily. It is PLEASCoG.

*P*ride
*L*ust
*E*nvy
*A*nger
*S*lothfulness
*Co*vetousness
*G*reed

Note that every one of these sins represents an emotional state or attitude. Absalom let his thoughts turn into the emotional attitudes of pride, anger, envy, covetousness, and greed. Perhaps he was also slothful. (Weighing one's hair every day hardly strikes me as noble work.) I suppose you could say he lusted after his father's throne—and wives—as well.

Absalom, in short, was not a spiritreneur. True spiritreneurs, like Jesus, set their hearts and minds on the kingdom of God, and take a disciplined approach toward doing so. Wise emotional investments don't just happen. They require daily choices and an act of will.

For me sometimes it's as simple as, "Do I turn on the TV or head for the computer?" Days when I don't choose wisely turn out to be wasted days. I consciously and constantly have to be asking myself, "What will I learn from reading this/watching this/doing this? How will this advance my mind or my spirit?" I know that I will suffer from poor reading or viewing choices.

The world offers us a daily dose of images that pollute the mind and spirit and bring it down. We spiritreneurs must put our mind to the plow. We must deliberately harness our energies to the higher things. Spiritreneurs—those of us who live what we love and love what we live—never lack for something to do. We simply have to choose to get off the couch and do it.

Perhaps David himself set a poor example for his son Absalom by lolling around on his roof at eventide, when he should have been engaged in battle. He let his mind and emotions invest in lust, and the rest is history.

All of us face those same temptations—some of us every day. Where shall I let my mind go today—tonight—right now?

Touch any of those "bases"—pride, lust, envy, anger, slothfulness, covetousness, greed—and you've put a foot in quicksand.

Spiritreneurs invest emotions wisely, just like Jesus did.

Questions

1. Which of the seven deadly sins are you facing right now?
2. Are you lingering—or leaping away?
3. How, specifically, did Jesus give us an example of overcoming sin both through salvation and choice?
4. Why must spiritreneurs invest emotions wisely?
5. Quick, name the seven deadly sins. Memorize them, so you can avoid them.

P

L

E

A

S

Co

G

Dear Lord,

You know all too well the temptations I face—to do the lesser thing, to descend and wallow in the lesser thoughts. Let me not be an "LCD" thinker—thinking and acting out the "lowest common denominator" of human behavior. Let me willfully choose the higher road—and give me the grace to do so.

> *Amen*

HE FINISHED WHAT HE STARTED

Here is someone who started to build and was unable to finish.

—Luke 14:30

It has long been one of my dreams to swim with the dolphins, so when the opportunity to do so arose on a recent trip to the Bahamas I signed up immediately. A boat took us out to a protected cove, and we were each carefully instructed as to what we could and could not do once we were in the water with these beautiful creatures.

The guide told us that dolphins are playful and curious, and that they may swim alongside us even when they're not "supposed" to. He told us they loved to be rubbed all over. The guide also pointed out a little bit of dolphin anatomy, and said not to rub dolphins below a certain point on their bellies. "Dolphins tend to get very excited about that," he said, "and we don't want you to start something you can't finish." The group laughed and laughed.

Spiritreneurs can be a lot like dolphins in our friendly, curious, and playful ways. Yet I also know the danger inherent in that, because we also can easily get excited about things that would be physically impossible for us to finish. As my friend Catherine would say, we have a tendency to overpromise and underdeliver.

I have done it and I've had it done to me, and I know it's a frustrating experience any way you look at it. I have learned—am learning—to be very careful about whose tummy I rub with my words, ideas, or promises.

About two years ago two young men took a train from Philadelphia to New York in order to meet me. They were launching a noble training program for underprivileged people and wanted me to help them. I gave them words of encouragement and support, and offered them both full scholarships to an upcoming Path training seminar. When I next heard back from a third party that they thought I was going to donate $200,000 to their cause, I was shocked, and had to hasten to clarify the exact terms and limitations of my support. Clearly, something I had said or implied in my enthusiasm had been mistranslated into a full-on commitment to launch their entire program. Fortunately, we were able to clear up the matter, but it was a good dolphin-rubbing lesson for me.

I was on the receiving end of a too promising "tummy rub" by a wonderful and successful businessperson who never met an idea he didn't like. After a four-hour conference in which he indicated a possible merger of our training efforts, I excitedly began to lay the groundwork with my staff. Apparently, his enthusiasm and commitment did not trickle down to the rest of his team, and when I flew in for a meeting with his

CEO, the man substituted an uninformed staff member so he, the CEO, could attend a budget meeting. This hugely successful businessperson's good intentions were never translated to the rest of the group. I was left high and dry, and had to trash about ninety days' worth of planning to go in another direction.

This man had started something he couldn't finish—not out of malice, but out of a desire to please. I would have been better off, really, if he had been rude to me. At least I would have been further along.

Proverbs warns about the insincere kisses of a flatterer. "Trustworthy are the blows of a friend, deceitful are the kisses from a foe" (Proverbs 27:6). Jesus warned about the importance of counting the costs before you launch a project—any project. Only a fool would not do so. Proverbs 25:14 reads, "Clouds and wind, but no rain: such is anyone whose promises are princely but never kept."

"And indeed, which of you here, intending to build a tower, would not first sit down and work out the cost to see if he had enough to complete it? Otherwise, if he laid the foundation and then found himself unable to finish the work, anyone who saw it would start making fun of him and say, "Here is someone who started to build and was unable to finish" (Luke 14:28–30).

Letting your yes be yes and your no be no is a very good way to run a business. In other words, don't rub every tummy you see just because it is presented to you. As the tour guide in the Bahamas said with a smile, "You don't want to start something you can't finish."

Jesus finished what he started.

Questions

1. When has someone made a promise to you that was not kept? What were the results?
2. When have you "overpromised and underdelivered"?
3. Why are spiritreneurs particularly vulnerable to this dangerous behavior?
4. What are some safeguards that you could build into your activities to help avoid misunderstandings?

Dear Lord,

You always finish what you start, and you know that your words have power. Let the same be said of me. Let me guard my words—especially my pleasing ones—so that no one is misled about my intentions. Help me remember that you take promises very seriously, and so should we.

Amen

HE WAS ACCOUNTABLE

It is to God, then, that each of us shall have to give an account.

—Romans 14:12

The four of us were sitting in a ballroom in the Bahamas, discussing what was happening as a result of the recent gathering of CEOs and leaders in the Caribbean. We began to discuss religious philosophies, weighing the judgmentalism and fundamentalism of some groups against the all-is-well-I-am-god types of thinking. Conference participant Marylyn Beaubien put it best. She said, "The one thing I see lacking today in so many lines of thinking is accountability."

Although Jesus came to give us power, he also intended that we be held accountable for it. Indeed, so much of what he said related to a final weighing in—of our words and deeds—of our use of time and talents. The question, then, we must ask is how are we—as spiritreneurs—measuring up? Are all our self-improvement courses teaching us to be more kind? As we approach the greatest amassing of wealth in history, are we "evolving" as spiritual beings, or just accumulating more toys?

I luxuriate and wallow in God's unconditional love, but am I becoming more loving—or simply "indulged"?

Part of accountability is changing how we measure success. In "Perspectives," a publication by the World Business Academy, the consultant Brenda Rarey challenges our current business measurement systems, stating that the current reporting system is based on agreements and assumptions made decades ago. She claims that we now have the ability, and responsibility, to build visionary measurement systems. And more and more spiritreneurs are doing just that—looking to measure more than how much profit is going to the bottom line.

One CEO of a faith-based hospital claims that every time her leadership team has a budget meeting, they are also required to attend a meeting centered around the hospital's spiritual mission. She declared, "I don't want money to be our only standard of measurement."

In the book *Chicken Soup for the Soul at Work* we learned that one of the largest printing companies in the world, Quad/Graphics, can produce a lot of waste. John Ines, their ecology manager, decided to go the extra mile in accounting for his company's behavior. Rather than viewing the Environmental Protection Agency as an adversary, Ines viewed them as a key and vital partner. "We live in this town," he said. "If we spew anything into the air, we'll all breathe it and so will our children. If we pollute the streams, we'll all be drinking it."

Among the changes Quad/Graphics made was perfecting soy-based inks to reduce pollution. Ironically, in their quest to "do right," they are also now doing extremely well, having become one of the world's largest suppliers of soy-based, biodegradable inks.

The Bible offers us many examples of the benefits of going that extra mile and the perils of stopping short. In Isaiah, shameful shepherds are condemned for neglecting their sheep. Jesus overturned the tables in the temple because the religious leaders were more concerned with counting money than prayers. Isaiah spoke often about the strict accounting measures God applies to careless shepherds.

In his final prayer in John 17 Jesus said, "These were your gifts, and you gave them to me. And I have not lost any of them."

Consider this tale of accountability, taken from an Associated Press newstory.

JUDGE'S DONATION SETTLES EVICTION CASE

When a suburban judge didn't feel the law offered him a fair solution for a deaf couple facing eviction, he took matters into his own hands: He paid their $250 back rent himself.

Appearing in Judge Donald McDonough's Fairfax, Va., courtroom, Deborah Morris and Louis Swann apparently faced almost certain eviction after lawyers for their landlord rejected a compromise on the overdue rent the couple said they were unable to pay.

Through a sign language interpreter, they told McDonough their financial problems Friday. He asked the landlord's lawyer, Andrew Lawrence, whether a settlement was possible. No, he said. McDonough sat silently for half a minute, then stood and strode to his chambers. When he returned, the judge leaned over his bench and passed two $100 bills and one $50 bill of his own money to the landlord's lawyer. He said: "Consider it paid."

The judge used his power here not only to command a solution, but to provide it. Just like Jesus did.

Jesus was accountable.

Questions

1. What does accountability mean to you?
2. Where in your life are you not being accountable?
3. What is the responsibility inherent in freedom?
4. What actions will you take today to be more accountable . . . to God?

Dear Lord,

I've fallen short. I've turned your windows into my mirrors, spun your gifts into gold for my own adorning, while indeed so many perish for lack of bread and water. Forgive me. Cleanse me. Accept me again—renew in me a right mind and spirit that I may act honorably and hear you say "Well done, good and faithful one, come dine with me tonight."

Amen

HE SUBMITTED HIS PLANS

You may make your plans. But God directs your actions.

—Proverbs 16:9

Things don't often turn out as planned—particularly in the world of the spiritreneur. Any spiritreneur you talk to could regale you with story after story of how they started out going in one direction, which seemed so sure, and ended up in entirely unfamiliar territory, even though they were praying the whole way.

I've laughingly shared with many friends my belief that God uses bait to get us hooked and then drags us where we're supposed to be. That is probably why some of the hottest strategic planners nowadays are not those with master's degrees in business administration or economics, but those who are the most well versed in chaos theory. Basically, chaos theory states that eventually what was unclear will be made clear, if you wait long enough (at least that's the way I see it). I remember learning in some college class the concept of entropy, which states that things left unattended always disintegrate (hence the need for human intervention).

Yet new prevailing theories are looking at organizations not as a series of charts and movable, predictable boxes, but as "organisms" that seem to have a life force within themselves, and therefore act unpredictably. It was not without surprise that I read a *USA Today* article chronicling the difficulties behind the merger of an organization founded by a man who teaches the importance of synergy—and another organization with a product line designed to help us prioritize and schedule our time. Both groups are leaders in their respective fields and this seemed like a smooth and obvious match for a merger. But the article detailed the unforeseen difficulties of getting two separate cultures to unite in happy matrimony. Apparently what the leaders had not foreseen was the number of feelings, customs, and practices that would have to be "untied" before they could be united in spirit as well as deed. (As I write this it occurs to me that if you move the "i" in "unite" one letter forward the word becomes "untie.")

The leaders took the bait of a sure deal and suddenly found themselves in unfamiliar territory. God is at work, again, humbling the works of humans, proving that true creation thrives in chaos—not conformity. I am certain that the leaders of those organizations prayed at length before their merger, and I'm certain that they landed smack dab in the middle of God's will even in the midst of their reported chaos. Apparently there were new and important lessons to be learned.

Let's face it. No fish is going to willingly be dragged to unfamiliar territory unless there is some tempting bait loaded on that hook. And the bait is usually "Follow Your Heart." Joseph didn't look at a young Mary and think, "Now there's a gal that's going to get pregnant before we even tie the knot. I think I'll pledge myself to her just for the heck of it." Joseph followed his heart in every way, and became not only a husband but a very important father as well.

Actress Julia Sweeney thought she was going to have a nice life in Los Angeles. Until her brother came down with cancer and her ailing mother came to live with her, and in the midst of this she came down with breast cancer. Out of this chaos came the best-selling book, movie, and Broadway play, *God Said "Ha!"* She understands the way God works.

"The human heart may plan a course. But it is Yahweh who makes the steps secure" (Proverbs 16:9).

When Jesus went daily to pray alone, he was offering all the events and his thoughts of the day up to God for scrutiny and guidance. Spiritreneurs must do the same.

Jesus submitted his plans.

Questions

1. Do you feel that God has ever "tricked" you? If so, why, how, and when?
2. Were you able to later see the good that came out of it?
3. Why do circumstances sometimes seem to lead one way only to end up taking us in another direction?
4. Was God able to make good anyway out of something that "went wrong"?
5. Name examples in history or in Scripture where this happened.

Dear Lord,
I trust you lead me in the paths of righteousness. Lead me,
especially, when the only step I see in front of me is one
that seems right to my heart.
Amen

HE KNEW EVERYONE HAS A RELATIVE

Whatever you have done to the least of these my brethren, you have done onto me.

—Matthew 25:40

My friend Linda and I walked eagerly out to the pasture to view her parents' new filly, born two weeks before. Tom and Jan Sterrett's Appaloosa horse ranch in Prescott, Arizona, also sported numerous geese, dogs, cats, pigeons, and goats. As Linda and I climbed though the corral and headed toward the mare and her foal, we both gasped to notice the trampled remains of a snake. "Wow—Lady (the mare) must have killed it before it got to the baby!" we theorized as we carefully lifted up the snake in gloved hands to bring it to her mom. "She'll be proud of Lady for being so brave," Linda said as we made our way back to the ranch house. "Mom, look what we found!" Linda yelled as we walked in the door triumphantly carrying the dead snake. Her mother took one look at the dangling remains and cried, "Betty? Is that you? Oh, no—poor baby!" Jan actually began to weep as she gently took the snake's dead body into her hands.

It turns out that Betty was Jan's pet king snake who had been kept in the barn to help control the rodent population. Linda and I stood speechless as Jan took Betty's body silently out to the oak tree to prepare for a funeral. Far from being participants in a triumph of horse good over snake evil, Linda and I found ourselves cast in the role of messengers of bad news and pallbearers. An innocent member of the family had been slain in a terrible misunderstanding—just because of the shape of its body. It was there, at Tom and Jan's Arizona ranch, that I learned that *everyone* has a relative—even snakes.

Jesus understood this when he called us brothers and sisters. Jesus understood this when he called the wind and seas to obey him, and noticed with great sadness a sparrow that had fallen to the ground. He told the hard-hearted Pharisees that "if you do not praise me, the very rocks and trees shall do so." All of creation is indeed related to God.

So how and why do we try so hard to label ourselves as "other"? I am white—you are black. Can this really make you "other" than me? Jesus prayed that we would be one, even as he and the Father are one. What must we do to end this illusion that we can be better than someone else—more holy, more pure? That our failings are all in the family while theirs expose and doom them to hell? Even Satan once sat at the family table before he decided to be better than God, different from God, and became a definite "other." But what is the relevance of "relatedness" to spiritreneurs?

It is a principle which when understood will drastically change your relationships and your ways of doing business.

You will begin to see that every action you take is significant . . . that there are no such things as big and little accounts, that each and every customer is somehow related to
you, and to many other very important people.

I spoke once at the Black Executive Management Retreat
and met a man there named Joseph Jones. I said, "My brother
is named Joe Jones—so you must be my brother, too." He
smiled and said, "I probably am." As he turned to go to his
next meeting he said, "You know, at one time in the Garden of
Eden everyone was named Jones. But then sin came, and
everybody had to scatter and take different names." He
laughed a hearty laugh as we waved good-bye, this tall handsome black executive who was, somehow, my brother.

St. Francis of Assisi used to speak to Brother Wolf and
Sister Dove. The animals responded to him because he saw
their "relative" importance to God.

As a spiritreneur I will do well to understand—and believe—that everything is relative. You can't hurt one thing
without hurting someone else invisible behind it.

Then the King will say to those on his right, "Come, you who
are blessed by my Father, take your inheritance, the kingdom
prepared for you since the creation of the world. For I was hungry and you gave me something to eat, I was thirsty and you
gave me something to drink, I was a stranger and you invited
me in, I needed clothes and you clothed me, I was sick and you
looked after me, I was in prison and you came to visit me."

The righteous will answer him, "Lord, when did we see you
hungry and feed you, or thirsty and give you something to
drink? When did we see you a stranger and invite you in, or

needing clothes and clothe you? When did we see you sick or in prison and visit you?

"Whatever you have done to the least of these, you have done to me" (Matthew 25:39–40).

Jesus knew everyone has a relative.

Questions

1. Do you see everyone as having a relative?
2. If not, how would having this perspective change the way you treated others?
3. How is the concept of "others" being played out in destructive ways?
4. What do you think Jesus meant when he prayed we all would be one, even as he and the Father are one?

Dear Lord,

Let me see all things as your creations, and thus related to me. Help me treat everyone with dignity and respect, especially the least in the world. It's the least I can do for you.

Amen

HE DIDN'T TRY TO HIDE FROM
THE WINEMAKER

He was lost, and now is found.
—Luke 15:24

The story of Gideon is one of the more remarkable examples of transformation in Scripture. The Israelites were under attack, and Gideon was hiding under a wine vat, thinking that surely no enemy would think to look for him there. Gideon wanted safety above all else. He wanted to escape the din of battle and the cries of the people as village after village was sacked and burned. He didn't want the light of reality—he wanted the damp, dark, sweet-smelling recesses of a place where the world would pass him by.

But Gideon forgot that you cannot hide from the winemaker, so it wasn't long before a giant hand lifted the lid off his hole and a thundering voice cried out, "The Lord is with you, man of valor!"

"Say what?" Gideon replied, perhaps thinking to himself, "Did I drink too much of this stuff before I climbed in here?"

Again the voice called out, "Go in the strength you have and save Israel!" Gideon, to be sure he was hearing from God, asked, "If it is really you, please give me a sign." And he got one (Judges 6:1–16).

Brian Anderson, a poet and artist from Indiana, writes, "I prayed for a sign. And then an angel in black tights came and said, 'You can begin now.' And I asked the angel 'Is this my sign?' And all I heard was laughter. . . ." God the winemaker will find you.

Like Gideon, Brian and Jonah and Moses and Mary and Peter all learned you cannot hide from the winemaker. So you might as well say "yes" and get on with it.

Perhaps you are a student, hiding out in the university library. Perhaps you are a worker in a factory, hiding out in the evenings with your remote control. Perhaps you are a mother, hiding out in your long To Do list. Perhaps you are a CEO hiding out in your multiple millions of shares. Perhaps you are a business owner, hiding out in your fear of growth. Perhaps you are a writer, hiding out in "The Formula" for success. Banker, butcher, candlestickmaker, God knows where you are—and is even now lifting the lid off your little hiding space and saying, "Hello! I know you're in there! Come on out. We've got work to do."

One place we all hide out is in our past. As long as we're looking in the rearview mirror we might miss the angel standing there, holding out a big "Welcome Home" sign. We forget that God is in the transformation business. We forget that we are being called to be more than we've ever been. We forget that God can reach us at our lowest, loneliest point, and take us by the hand and turn us into heroes. You see, Gideon went on to win one of the most magnificent battles in Jewish history. He picked up his sword, recruited an army, and sent the vanquishers running home, their tails between their legs.

In the beautiful book *Traveling Mercies* by Anne Lamott, she writes about a long, bumpy ride that reaches a point where she slides off a cliff of despair. She had just gotten an abortion and had gone home by herself to recover. Soon she began to hemorrhage. The drugs she had taken and the loss of blood began to leave her light-headed. She thought that surely she was going to die, and at that point she didn't care.

She said she was aware of a presence in the room. She lifted up her head and looked across the bed and there she saw him—Jesus, wearing blue jeans, sitting on his haunches. At first she thought she was delirious. She looked again. He was still there—radiating a silent love and acceptance, challenge and concern. She said, "I'd rather die than become a Jesus freak!" She recovered from her loss of blood, but the presence wouldn't leave her. She said it followed her like a silent cat. "I was determined not to feed it, because once you feed a cat it stays." But finally as she was walking along she cursed and then said, "Oh, all right. You can come in now." And he did. The winemaker had found her.

So it is that this easygoing wandering-soul hippie began a journey that led her to speaking about God's mercy to people all across the world. Anne Lamott went from hiding from the winemaker to pouring out his wine. She became a spiritreneur simply by saying "yes."

On my recent trip to Jerusalem, I was stunned to learn that the tomb many archaeologists believe to be Jesus's tomb is located in a vineyard.

How appropriate. Even in his death, Jesus did not hide from the winemaker.

Questions

1. Where are you hiding out from God?
2. What is it you're afraid of?
3. What is the booming voice saying you must do?
4. If you were to pick up your sword, what would it look like?

Dear Lord,

I've been hiding from you—not returning phone calls, avoiding the places where I think you'll be. And yet I can't even speak a word but you know what it is. So I'm reaching out my hand and asking you to lift me up. I'm getting cramps in my soul from squatting so long. Come on, Lord. I'm ready. Let's go.

Amen

HE KNEW HIS HERDS

Know your flocks' condition well, take good care of
your herds; for riches do not last forever, crowns do not
hand themselves on from age to age.

—Proverbs 27:23–24

Flocks and herds were the foundation of the Jews' prosperity, so throughout the Old Testament we are presented with a clear portrait of what a good shepherd is, and how one behaves. For example, good shepherds watch their flock at night, they chase away predators, they gather the weak ones in their arms, they go looking for that which is lost.

The Lord spoke strong words in Scripture against shepherds who fattened themselves and cared nothing for their herds. "This is what the Sovereign Lord says: Woe to the shepherds of Israel who only take care of themselves! Should not shepherds take care of the flock? You eat the curds, clothe yourselves with the wool and slaughter the choice animals, but you do not take care of the flock. You have not strengthened the weak or healed the sick or bound up the injured. You have not brought back the strays or searched for the lost. You have ruled them harshly and brutally" (Ezekiel 34:1–4).

It is easy in our hurried society to get so caught up in counting the sheep that we lose sight of their condition. Tales are too common of doctors who go into surgery and amputate the wrong foot, or take out an appendix when a hernia repair had been scheduled. Somebody forgot to check the charts or, better yet, the actual condition of the patients themselves.

A bad foot versus a good foot should be obvious even to an untrained eye, much less to someone who is a highly trained professional. Yet I see in business how easy it is for us not to know the condition of our herds, just the quantity of them.

A company I once consulted for was in a rush to "go public." In an effort to fatten their bottom line they began acquiring medical facilities at the rate of two per month. The CEO I worked with had taken the job because of his real desire to make changes in the way treatments were being delivered to the elderly.

When he realized that the stockholders' only driving force was to add facilities, not improve patient care, he quit. "I guess you could say I wanted to be a shepherd, when what they wanted was a stockyard acquisitions expert." He now works out of his home, taking his kids to and from school. "At least I can tell you exactly how and where they are now," he said with a smile.

Computers have not necessarily made this easier. We decided to cut our mailing list by purging everyone who had not responded to our mailings over the last two years. Dee then decided to double-check some of the names that were being cut. I had to laugh when Dee said, "Laurie, you, your mom, and Catherine were in the 'purge' group as people who had not responded to any of our mailings."

"Yeah, what a group of deadbeats! Save the postage. Cut us off!"

Mom, Catherine, and I (I hope) are central to the heart of the organization. If Dee hadn't been an alert shepherd, we might have been tossed over the cliff with other sheep that had no signs of a pulse.

The social implications of not knowing the condition of your herd was never brought home more tragically than in the case of the two boys who went on a shooting rampage and killed thirteen people in Littleton, Colorado. The fact that responsible adults were unaware of the boys' obsession with guns, violence, and video games like Doom sadly pointed to shepherds who didn't really know the condition of their sheep. Shortly after the killings there was a news feature about a mother who had been worried about her son's loss of interest in school, and who secretly taped his phone conversations and searched his room. When she found out he was actually dealing drugs, she intervened and placed him in a residential care facility. Today, he is off drugs and back to living a normal life. He credits his "nosy" mom for actually saving his life.

I've worked with doctors who couldn't tell you the names of their last five patients. I've worked with small business owners who eagerly purchase names for new mailing lists when they haven't even recontacted their old customers in the last three years. Good shepherds know the condition of the herds they have before they go merging with others.

"I know my sheep and my sheep know me" (John 10:14).
Jesus knew his herds.

Questions

1. Why is it that a spiritreneur must know the condition of his or her herd?
2. Name three possible consequences of not knowing your herd's condition—economically, socially, and spiritually.
3. What can you do to assure that you personally know the condition of your flocks?
4. Could God praise you as a good and faithful shepherd?

Dear Lord,
Help me to be a wise and faithful shepherd, keeping watch over my flocks by day and especially whenever darkness is nigh. Help me be able to say, as Jesus did, "I know my own, and my own know me." Let my voice be soothing— and very familiar—to each one of them.

Amen

HE DID SWEAT THE SMALL STUFF

*Since you have proved faithful in a very little matter,
you shall govern much.*

—Luke 19:17

I recently saw a special on the Discovery Channel about the animals of the Kalahari Desert. It was a fascinating documentary of the night and day creatures that inhabit a unique part of the world. I found myself cooing in delight when I saw a mother porcupine emerge from a burrow, followed by two little miniature porcupines. They were an exact replica of their mother, scaled down to one-fifth the size. I thought "Wouldn't it be cute to have a baby porcupine on the ranch?" A split second later logic set in. "Are you crazy? Their little miniature tails pack a powerful wallop."

Spiritreneurs all have baby porcupines running around. We tolerate or indulge them because the problems they pose seem so minor. A sloppy report. An unchecked document. An order hastily thrown together. A catty remark about a coworker. A curse word in the lunch room. All baby porcupines, really. They're no big deal. But baby porcupines grow up to be big porcupines, and their quills when released can be multiple, painful, and deadly if left unattended.

When I lived in the mountains I constantly had to pull porcupine quills out of my dog Shiloh's nose. The quills have little hooks on the ends so you can't pull them straight out. If you leave even one of them in, your dog's muzzle can get infected and then, if untreated, can cause it to starve to death. Forest rangers say they've seen many coyotes who starved to death because of porcupine quills.

My grandfather used to tell me that a small leak can sink a big ship. A little lapse in character here or there, a little white lie left unattended, can have devastating effects—no matter how insignificant it seems at the time.

A leader must be vigilant about baby porcupines. A racial slur that's allowed to cross the lips of a child can lead to a lifetime of bigotry. Slacking off and missing a detail in your work can lead to big-time failure. Proverbs 18:9 says, "Whoever is slack in his work is blood-brother to the destroyer." Baby porcupines follow big mothers.

Kids who break windows in one town are treated as potential serious offenders. Rather than receive a slap on the wrist they are immediately put into a youth-at-risk intervention program, and their parents, too, are called in for counseling.

A friend of mine was attending a church brunch with an elderly woman whose two sons are currently in prison—both serving life sentences for murder. The conversation got around to how much more challenging some of the women found it to raise sons than daughters.

The elderly woman turned to my friend and said proudly, "My boys never gave me an ounce of trouble." My friend said it was all she could do not to spit out her cake laughing. Ah, the blind love and devotion of a mother's heart! Unfortunately, spiritreneurs better have someone around who is willing to discipline the small problems before they became big ones. Felons aren't created overnight. Neither is bankruptcy or divorce.

A television ad I saw recently made me laugh. It showed Noah and his wife checking off the animals as they entered the ark two by two. "Ostriches." "Check." "Peacocks." "Check." "Rhinoceros." "Check." "Termites." "Check." There is a pause as a look of horror crosses Noah's face. "Termites?!" he yells. "Call [XYZ] Pest Control!" In the final scene the [XYZ] truck is shown being driven onto the ark. No wonder Noah survived the flood. He didn't let little problems grow into big ones.

In his journey to save the world, Jesus still took the time to notice baby birds and little girls and flowers swaying in the breeze. By getting his team to notice little things and pay attention to small details, he was teaching them the larger principles.

"To those who are faithful with a little—more will be given" (Matthew 25:23).

Jesus did sweat the small stuff.

Questions

1. Which little porcupines are you tolerating in your organization, thinking they're too small to do much harm?
2. Can you think of an example when a small problem you left attended turned into a big one?
3. Name three trait(s) that are required to maintain standards of excellence.

4. Who most exemplifies those three traits in your life?
5. How are you going to make sure your ark has no termites?

Dear Lord,
Give me low to zero tolerance for leaks, termites, and baby
porcupines that waddle near playpens. Help me, indeed,
sweat the small stuff.
Amen

HE CHOSE HIS FRIENDS CAREFULLY

Blessed is the one who does not walk in the counsel of the wicked or stand in the way of sinners, or sit in the seat of mockers.

—Psalms 1:1

Perhaps you've seen the T-shirt on couples walking hand in hand. The shirt reads "I'M WITH STUPID"—and underneath is an arrow pointing toward the other person. Of course, the implication is that the person with Stupid is even stupider because s/he recognizes the ignorance of the other person and yet chooses to remain.

Blaming someone else for your mistakes is literally the oldest trick in the book. "The woman you put here with me—she gave me some fruit from the tree, and I ate it." The woman said, "The serpent deceived me, and I ate" (Genesis 3:12). God cut Adam and Eve no slack in the deal. Both were punished.

As my friend Mike Regan pointed out to me during an impromptu Bible study on the way to the airport, the sick man who was lying by the pool in John 5:4 said he couldn't get into the healing waters because there was nobody there to lift him in. Jesus asked him if he wanted to be healed. Perhaps he sensed in this man's "blaming" and "victimhood" a desire to remain unable to walk. Therefore, a direct question was in order. Jesus did not say, "Call your friends and they will help you." He did not say, "Oh, you poor fellow. I can see that you are alone here (except for me, my disciples, and the few hundred other people that gather by the pool)." Jesus asked him a direct question, and then gave him a direct command: "Get up and walk."

Jimmy, the son of a wealthy landowner, was visiting in a tavern, talking to a young woman who was apparently with someone else. This someone else proceeded to take the young law student out of the bar and beat him senseless. Bloodied, indignant, and certain that he could file a lawsuit, Jimmy called home and asked his father to pull out the stops in getting this guy arrested. His father's response, as was that of his highpowered attorney, was that "once you walk into a place like that, you assume the risk of all its patrons." The lesson for Jimmy was that the judge was not going to favor "Stupid" just because he ended up getting a black eye from someone he claimed was stupider. As spiritreneurs we must guard well the company we keep, and the spaces we inhabit.

I once took on a client who was foul-mouthed and abusive (to others) because he had a terrific product to promote and our advertising agency needed the cash flow. I was later startled to learn that he had actually been kicked out of an entire state by the attorney general—but had used his charm and carpetbag to set up shop on the West Coast. By the time I was able to extricate myself and the agency from this man I had mud all over my face. Who was more stupid? Him—for acting the way he did—or me for not checking out his references?

When you find yourself in a bad situation, or tangled up with someone who's starting to drag you down, the best and quickest thing you can do is to free yourself at once. Proverbs 6:13 states: "If you have co-signed a note with a fool, go—run to the judge, and do all you can to get yourself free of it."

You also, as an employer, have an obligation to your customers not to hire a fool. "He who hires an incompetent worker is like an untamed archer, wounding everyone who passes" (Proverbs 26:10).

Martha S. Wilkinson, executive vice president for Nordstroms, is adamant about screening people carefully during the hiring process. She says, "People who don't want to sell will never make it in our system. If you don't understand how important the relationship with the customer is, you just won't do well here."

I can recall several situations now where I failed to screen employees or new hires. Thinking myself too busy to meet the new people, I was aghast when I did finally meet our new intern, "Betty." The first time I saw her was on TV. She was sitting at a desk with my company name emblazoned beneath her. Betty had volunteered to work the phone lines for the 5 to 7 P.M. shift for the local telethon. Not bad. Except that she was wearing a tight knit blouse displaying lots of "leverage," as she called it. She was chewing gum and giggling and when the phones weren't ringing she was blowing kisses to the audience.

That was the last time I let the guys in the art department

select our summer interns. Fortunately, only a few of my clients saw her on TV, so the damage was minimal.

Scripture makes clear that having weak friends or employees is dangerous. In heaven, there are no matching T-shirts. You will be evaluated by your own designs. "I shall judge each of you by what *you* do" (Ezekiel 33:20).

Jesus chose his friends carefully.

Questions

1. Who are you using as an excuse?
2. How much time do you spend complaining about others?
3. Can you recall a situation where you made a poor relationship choice—and what it cost you? Who ended up looking "stupid"?

Dear Lord,

Help me realize that there is no blame in heaven—and none effective on earth. Let me know that I am responsible for my own actions, and that there are places where you alone can be my guide. Forgive me my black and blue bruises suffered at the hands of people I chose to be around. Help me make better choices.

Amen

HE KEPT HIS MAPS CURRENT

New wine must be poured into new wineskins.

—Luke 5:38

Millions of Americans and Chinese were shocked when NATO mistakenly bombed the Chinese Embassy during their air raids on Yugoslavia. Apparently, the devastating mistake occurred because the CIA was working off old maps. A political cartoon in the *National Catholic Reporter* showed a flying ace in goggles manning a biplane, trying to read a huge, ancient map entitled "The Ottoman Empire." The letters NATO were proudly emblazoned on the side of the plane.

A once-in-a-lifetime mistake, perhaps? Tell that to the families of the skiers in Italy whose lives were cut short when a low-flying American jet sliced the cable on their ski lift, causing scores of people to tumble to their deaths. The military brass tried to blame the incident on a "hotdogging" pilot, yet their prosecution plan fell apart when the defense showed that the maps provided to the pilot and crew showed no ski slopes, ski resort, or ski lifts on them. The military's response: "The pilots should have known."

Spiritreneurs cannot afford to make decisions based on dusty old maps. We must be people who are aware of the times, prepared to move with them.

Once Joseph became convinced that his wife was indeed carrying the child destined to be King of the Jews, he could have blindly rested on the fact, claiming his inheritance even as Herod's soldiers were bearing down on Jerusalem. When Joseph had a dream that told him to take his wife and future son deep into enemy territory, in Egypt, Joseph obeyed. He kept his maps and plans current and saved his family.

A friend who is a corporate consultant says with a sigh that one major worldwide religious organization could never survive in a corporate environment because their leadership sticks to old maps rather than keeping current ones. "Consider their recruiting policies—gender-exclusive. Consider their response to customers—we are always right. Consider their response time—four hundred years to clear Galileo of heresy for saying the earth was not the center of the universe." Perhaps you could name other organizations that have these same "dusty map" problems.

What's true today on a map may not be true tomorrow.

Jesus understood that. In fact, he changed all the maps of his time. Essentially, what he was saying was "The way to God is not through killing sheep and pigeons—it is through me. God doesn't want burnt sacrifices—He wants you to treat others with kindness and respect. Before me, only Jews could know God. Now that I've come, heaven's doors are open to all who believe." Jesus was, in fact, a map maker.

In business, we see examples every day of leaders bombing embassies instead of arsenals. Just last week, for example, I went with my niece to a major department store to help her return a graduation gift. She had received a blouse that didn't fit and wanted to return it for a store credit. The price tag was still on it and it was in the department store gift box.

The woman at the counter frowned. "I'll have to call the manager to get approval," she said. Five minutes went by. The manager called back. The woman then asked my niece to provide her full name, address, telephone number, and Social Security number. At this point I stepped in and said, "Why are you treating her like she's a criminal to be traced? She's only returning a $35 blouse!" "Policy," said the clerk. We dutifully filled out all the forms, and then the clerk had to call for an assistant manager to OK the forms we had filled out. I asked, "Why is this interrogatory behavior a store policy?"

"Well," said the clerk, "we once had an employee turn in a shoplifted item for credit."

"I see," I replied. "And when did this happen?"

"I think it was in 1976," said the assistant manager, who approved what was now a stack of paperwork so my niece could receive her credit.

One foul incident has shaped an entire negative policy. This department store is operating off old maps.

One businessman from Florida I know said, "Tell me about keeping current. My partner Ernie predicts the Internet is just a fad. He still wants to sell books door to door!"

Jesus said, "It has been written, but I say . . ." In other words, he was updating the software. "Do men pour new wine into old wineskins?" Jesus asked in Matthew 9:17. Of course not. "Do not conform to the standards of the world but let God change you inwardly by a renewing of your mind" (Romans 12:2).

Jesus kept his maps current.

Questions

1. How current is/are your business maps?
2. Are you operating from dusty data?
3. How often does the map in your industry change?
4. Are you on top of—or being affected by—changes?

Dear Lord,
You see all—know all. Nothing is a surprise to you. Give
me your gift of discernment and help me always to seek
current information.
        Amen

THE LOVE:
LIVING THE VISIONARY LIFE
OF THE SPIRITRENEUR

In Phase Four you begin to encounter bliss on a regular basis. You now recognize landmarks that were promised to you during the early vision you received in your Launch phase. The milk and honey begins to flow, and the lion of your drive and ambition finally lies down with the lamb of peace.

Dream and reality, faith and grace, rest and waking become one. Like an eagle soaring on an invisible updraft, you can see clearly the valleys beneath you that you thought would be your downfall during the Lurch. Oh, how far you have come from those first frightening lessons, you realize as you soar.

You stretch out your wings and feel the sun on your back. You are grateful, alive, comforted by the knowledge that this is where you were meant to be, doing what you are doing. This flight is a reflection of God, and you who were created in God's image. You are loved and challenged and desired, and working, in flight, in delight, in power.

You are a spiritreneur, soaring high for all to see, feeling the joy of God in your wings, inspiring others with your daring. You have finally embraced the Love in all you see and do.

HE STAYED FASCINATED

Cain went out from the Lord's presence and lived in the land of Nod.

—Genesis 4:16

Maybe another reason God got so upset with Adam and Eve was because before they ate the fruit of knowledge, they had been fascinated by everything.

God, what were we thinking when
you made waterfalls?
Where did you get the color
scheme for the toucan?
How is it that birds always
find their way home?

Questions such as these might have peppered their walks together in the cool of the evening, much to God's delight.

But after they ate from the "tree of knowledge," this behavior changed from fascination to fear and shame, to boredom. Where else could they go but into the valley—a place where nobody cared, nobody worshipped, nobody listened. A place where no one ever asked any questions.

My friend Beau Black once told me that he thinks God put him on this earth simply to be "amazed."

"It's a full-time job when you think about it," he said. "The world is so full of wondrous things."

Perhaps the most stunning example I know of a person staying fascinated was when a multimillionaire friend of mine rather cheerfully announced one day that he was being audited by the IRS. Again. "Charles," I said, "doesn't that upset you? Most people fear audits worse than death!"

"Oh no, I actually enjoy them," he said. "I have nothing to hide, and when we sit down together with the IRS agent and pore over all my businesses, I always learn something new. It's a great education!" he said, and meant it. He was fascinated by the whole process.

When my mother went in for her angioplasty you'd have thought she was a science writer. She kept asking so many questions about both how things were done and the people in the room that my brother actually begged them to put her completely out. Mom breezed through the procedure and emerged not as a victim of heart disease but as a newly initiated and deeply informed member of the Phoenix, Arizona, medical community. The fact that she could have died during the operation never crossed her mind. She wouldn't let it. She felt she was there to learn, and turned the experience into a fascinating education.

As part of a business course requirement I was on a weekend retreat with people whose world views turned out to be very different from mine. In desperation I called a friend and whispered, "I can't take it! I feel at any moment they're going to take my textbook out, find out that I have underlined passages that are different from theirs, and stomp me to death on the stage amid shouts of traitor! I have to get out of here!" Mary told me to take ten deep long breaths, and then reminded me that I really wanted and needed this course. She then said, "Laurie, why don't you pretend you are a reporter who's been assigned to cover the retreat? Don't think of these people as enemies. Be fascinated by who they are. Learn what they think and why they think that way."

I tried it, and it worked. So now, whenever I find myself in a painful situation, I switch into the "fascinated reporter" mode, and it nearly always calms me down. One reason spiritreneurs succeed is because we are curious about everything. By constantly probing and asking questions, we uncover opportunities, treasures, and insights that less curious people pass by. Jesus was fascinated by God's effortless work in nature, and advised us to consider it too.

True leaders stay fascinated watching a process unfold rather than fearing the end results. What I can't understand is how anyone can resist being fascinated. In fact, it worries me how many have blinded themselves to the world's wonders.

I had some extra time between media appointments in New York so I asked the limo driver to drive me around some of the outlying areas. A native New Yorker for fifty years, he was a gruff sort who didn't seem to want to chat much. We drove into an area called Yonkers, which was full of quaint shops and villages. "What can you tell me about Yonkers?" I asked.

He replied, "Yonkers ain't got nothin' goin' for it. Never has—never will."

Just then we drove past a historical marker that read "Yonkers. Established 1608." "This town has been here for three hundred and ninety years!" I said. "Surely something interesting must have happened here."

"Look, lady," the driver said. "They ain't got no ball clubs, so why should I know from Adam what they've done?" And that was the end of that.

Here was a man in the hospitality industry who was clearly not fascinated by his surroundings—surroundings which others paid him to drive through. He had allowed a job that could offer endless fascination to become a dead-end task of dreariness.

If you would remain in Paradise, simply stay fascinated. And then God will always be walking at your side.

"Consider the lilies of the field, how they grow . . ." (Matthew 6:28).

Jesus stayed fascinated.

Questions

1. What still fascinates you?
2. Are you a jaded couch potato—being fed information through tubes—or are you out exploring, turning over rocks to look for bugs?
3. How could staying fascinated benefit you in your career? In your marriage? In your family life?
4. How interested are you, really, in things outside yourself?

Dear Lord,
Give me the joy of wonder again in your marvelous world,
in your marvelous deeds—among your awesome people.
Open my eyes that I may see all that you have that de-
lighted me. Remind me, once again, I am not the center of
the universe—merely an actor in it.

Amen

HE ALWAYS WASHED WITH TIDE

*You know how to interpret the appearance of the sky,
but you cannot interpret the sign of the times.*

—Matthew 16:3

In studying the events of Jesus' life, I am always intrigued by
his awareness of the importance of God's timing. He seemed
not to put too much stock in the outer appearances of events,
but viewed them rather in a continuum of God's larger plan.
For example, he was not impressed when the crowds hailed
him as their king and laid down carpets of palm fronds for
him. He knew that soon they would be weaving him a crown of
thorns from a very different kind of tree. He didn't act startled
at Peter's assertion that he would always be faithful to him,
even though he knew that soon Peter would deny him three
times. Nor did he fail to wash the feet of Judas, despite knowing that soon those feet would be running toward the very people who would arrest him. So I like to think that in all things,
Jesus washed with Tide—God's tide—aware of the ebb and
flow, the rise and fall, the incessant motion that is life.

Spiritreneurs must also remember to wash with that tide. The writer in Ecclesiastes said it so beautifully: "To everything there is a time, and a purpose under heaven. A time to build up, a time to tear down, a time to reap, a time to sow, a time to embrace, a time to refrain from embracing" (Ecclesiastes 3:5).

One reason so many of us are not resting is because we have lost touch with the natural rhythms of life itself. Thomas Cherny, a friend of mine who lives in Austria, described to me the awe he felt watching an eclipse from atop a hill in his hometown of Graz. He said thousands of people had gathered to watch the miracle of the sun and the moon lining up and casting a shadow across the earth. He said the crowd was milling anxiously in anticipation, yet as the moon actually covered the sun in those few moments of celestial harmony, a silence fell over the entire city.

He said, "It was as if we realized, if only for a moment, how much we depend on the rhythms of God for our very existence."

A line in a recent presidential inaugural bothered me, when we were urged to "force the spring." It made me think of artificially red tomatoes, or apples which I buy out of season just because they are the right color, hoping against hope they will have the crispness that only comes in September and October, no matter what the label. As spiritreneurs our tendency is to try to force the spring, yet we must remember to heed the seasons—God's seasons—and respect them.

Recently an article in a media magazine touted the fall of one of the major movie studio executives. Hired by the new CEO because of a string of successes at another studio, this "genius" had to watch several of his subsequent movie projects fail at the box office. Inevitably and predictably he was fired. When asked by a reporter how he felt about the axing, he said, "I learned years ago that when you're hot, you're about to get cold, and when you're cold, you're about to get hot." Sure enough, right after he was forced to leave, four of the movie projects started under his supervision became mega-hits. But by then he was gone.

The shortsighted CEO who fired him had not learned to wash with, or watch, the tide.

In a group teleconference I had, one of the *Jesus CEO* University students, Paula, lamented that she was "drifting." For the first time in her life she was between major projects and was feeling uncomfortable about her lack of attachment in the business world. A month later when we spoke again, she shared that her father had suffered a stroke, and she was the only one of the children who was free to care for him and supervise his rehabilitation. "Now I know why God had me in such a free space," she said in awe through her tears. "He was preparing me to take care of my father." We were once again made aware of the divine order that serves and supports us all.

I wrestle with God all the time. When the tide is low I yearn for the days when it was crashing around my shoulders. When the tide is so heavy and thick that I am sure the next wave is going to carry me away, I rush toward the shore where the waves cannot reach me.

Like a cat who always wants to be on the other side of the door that it is on, I am constantly meowing at God—either about the heaviness of my workload, or about how nothing seems to be happening.

Have you lost a key client? Your bid for that big contract came in second? Maybe it seems like every person you ever knew rolled out of town with the last dust storm. Remember, when you're cold, you're about to get hot again.

How wise we can be, we spiritreneurs, as we walk along the shores of life. After all, we have learned to respect the rhythms of life. Just like Jesus.

He always washed with Tide.

Questions

1. Where in your life are you trying to "force the spring," or push things prematurely?
2. How can you be aware of the natural rhythms of life to increase your energy and your effectiveness?
3. Can you tell the difference between an in-season, and out-of-season, apple?
4. Do you think your customers can?

Dear Lord,
Help me to remember that your timing is always perfect . . . that you gave us night to rest and the day to work, and the Sabbath to enjoy both. Both the darkness and the light are all a part of your perfect plan, as am I.

Amen

HE LEFT IT ALONE

Get thee behind me, Satan.
　　　　　—Luke 4:8

Satan offered Jesus many "gifts" in the wilderness. The gift of immediate gratification, the gift of acknowledgment, the gift of worldly splendor. Jesus touched not one of them, armed with a sense of mission and a deep knowledge of Scripture. Jesus "left it alone."

Spiritreneurs must know when, where, and how best to use the energy we've been given. A master craftsman works with nuances of detail—a touch here versus a hard rubbing there. Yet many spiritreneurs I've met feel that they must apply the same amount of effort, pressure, and time to every client and every deal.

This is not what Jesus did as he made his rounds. He knew which person to lift up, and which ones to put down. He also knew that some things needed to be left alone.

This principle came to light for me recently when I discovered a very fat toad sitting on the sidewalk by my rose garden. My friend Irene and my godsons Jacob and Joseph were visiting at the time. I said to Irene in a worried tone, "I wonder if I should move the toad outside the gate. That way the dogs won't bother him. But if I do, then he might hop out into the road and the cars will get him. Or I could put him out by the pasture, but then the horses might step on him. What to do, what to do . . ." It was then that I heard six-year-old Joseph whisper to his little brother, "I think Laurie needs to join the Leave It Alone Club!" His mother and I burst out laughing at his practical advice. Obviously, the toad had done well enough on his own. What made me think my human intervention would save him?

There are times in business when we spiritreneurs should also join the Leave It Alone Club. Like when someone starts gossiping about a competitor. Or when there is an argument going on between two staff members. Perhaps someone invites us to accept a favor from a less than reputable person . . . or a coworker slips us a flirtatious smile that says, "I'm all yours if you want me."

The temptations faced by spiritreneurs range from the minute, such as the white lie about when an order will be ready, to the grandiose, such as the recent $15 billion money laundering scam uncovered in Russia. When a spiritreneur reaches out to touch something that s/he knows should be left alone, the consequences can be severe. Like the well-meaning characters in the *Tales of Uncle Remus* who tried to remove Tar Baby by touching him, we too can find ourselves stuck in the middle of the very situation we sought to improve.

I'm reminded of a self-proclaimed Christian actress who engaged in an affair with a married multimillionaire because she said she wanted to convert him. Ultimately it was her reputation—not his—that was ruined. When she saw that handsome married business associate, she would have been better off if she had just turned around and sought membership in the Leave It Alone Club.

Our time, our energy, our reputation are precious. There are some deals we shouldn't touch . . . some people we don't need to meet . . . some appointments we don't need to keep . . . some opportunities we must ignore.

Peter, knowing what awaited Jesus in Jerusalem, said, "Jesus, don't go." And Jesus said, "Get thee behind me, Satan . . . I must do my Father's will." Here was a chance suggested by a friend to take the lesser road. But Jesus looked at the key to false freedom that was being offered to him, and decided to Leave It Alone.

Where would we all be if Adam and Eve had just ignored that tree? If only they, too, had joined the Leave It Alone Club.

When it came to sin and temptation, Jesus left it alone.

Questions

1. What are you being tempted to reach out and grab, even though your inner voice is telling you to leave it alone?
2. Give five examples of business failures caused by leaders who could not leave well enough alone.
3. What is really motivating a person who has to take every call, close every deal?

Dear Lord,
The essence of wisdom is knowing what to embrace and
what to leave behind. Give me your discernment in every
transaction I face, and every deal I make.

Amen

HE SLEPT

The Lord gives his beloved sleep.
　　　　　　—Psalm 127:2

Studies show that most Americans are sleep-deprived. The National Sleep Foundation calls it an epidemic of the "insufficient sleep syndrome." Single mothers. Dual-income families. Truck drivers. Teachers. Air traffic controllers. Politicians. Mechanics. Assembly line workers. Teenagers, especially. We all yearn for more sleep. But we can't seem to make the time. There is, after all, so much to be done . . . so much to be done . . . I'm exhausted, but this cup of Java will give me my second wind.

"The Lord gives his beloved sleep," read one of the Psalms.

Yet when I asked a group of pastors what their number one problem was, "exhaustion" was the almost unanimous response. When I asked them who they're working for, they replied in unison, "Jesus." I then asked them, after a long pause, "Did Jesus sleep?" "Yes," was the reply from one. "He slept quite well!" piped up another. "In fact, he could fall asleep in the middle of a storm!" yelled out a pastor from the back.

"And how could Jesus sleep, knowing there was so much work to do?" I asked the group again. There was a long silence.

"I propose that Jesus could sleep because he knew what his mission was, and he stuck to it. All the rest he entrusted to God," I said.

Spiritreneurs must remember that sleep is vital—sleep is good—sleep is to be sought and guarded as a precious well of your own energy reserves.

God rested on the seventh day and declared that we should too. It was a rule meant for our healing.

Yet we cannot rest when we serve other gods. Other gods do not allow sleep. If we are sleep-deprived perhaps we are serving the wrong god. In fact they threaten sleep as a curse. Who is your god—your true god? Success?—it never sleeps. Fame?—it cannot rest.

Our ignoring of the concept of rest is taking its toll. High schools and colleges are spending enormous sums of money to educate students who are too sleepy to take in or analyze information. Drowsy drivers cause roughly 100,000 auto accidents each year. Research commissioned by the U.S. Congress indicated that lack of sleep led to errors in critical thinking in three of the worst disasters in recent U.S. history: the *Challenger* explosion, the *Exxon Valdez* oil spill, and the near-meltdown at Three Mile Island.

Yet a Gallup survey reported that 46 percent of people suffering from sleep deprivation attribute it to job-related stress.

A quarter of those respondents believed it was not possible to achieve career success without sleep deprivation. Although eight hours is the minimum recommended sleep per night, *Fast Company* magazine reported that 33 percent of adults sleep less than six and a half hours a night; 62 percent of adults experience sleep problems at least two nights a week. And 45 percent of adults will sleep less in order to accomplish more. Martin Moore-Ede, M.D., author of *The 24-Hour Society: Understanding Human Limits in a World That Never Stops,* argues that "the ability to be creative lies in the frontal areas of the brain, and those are the areas that are most sensitive to sleep deprivation."

Jesus loved to sleep. And he lives to watch us sleep. A shepherd whose little lambs are at rest is one contented shepherd, singing softly to himself that all is well—will be well—now that the shepherd is nigh.

I never experienced God's love and grace as much as I did one day not too long ago as I was awakening from sleep. The dawn's light had just broken over the mountains when I found myself in that ethereal state between deep sleep and half awakening. For a few moments I hovered there, and as I did I felt as if I were nestled in the palm of God's hand. There was angels' breath all around me, and the feeling of rarefied, golden air. I had a sense of impending and ever-expanding well-being—and I could sense that I was being looked on with such deep, intense love that tears sprang to my eyes.

I hadn't even gotten up yet! I hadn't done anything good—how could I be receiving so much love, not as reward for doing, but simply for being?

In her book *Traveling Mercies,* Anne Lamott reminds us that William Blake wrote, "We are put here to learn to endure the beams of love."

In the beautiful book *Sabbath* by Wayne Muller, the author urges us to restore the sacred rhythm of rest. He includes a quote by Annie Dillard: "We are most deeply asleep at the switch when we fancy we control any switches at all. We sleep to time's hurdy-gurdy; we wake, if we ever wake, to the silence of God."

Jesus slept.

Questions

1. What is your attitude toward sleep? Do you crave it or resent it?
2. Do you sleep blissfully or fitfully?
3. Do you know how much sleep you need?
4. What is keeping you up at night?
5. Do you know your mission? If not, are you perhaps trying to live everyone else's?

Dear Lord,
Cradle me in the palm of your hand. Let me rest tonight—
calm in the knowledge of your love. Let angel's breath sing
me to sleep and your golden beams of love and grace
awaken me—fully rested—in the morning.

Amen

HE WAS NOT A PERFECTIONIST

Woe unto you who tithe down to the last mint leaf in
your garden, but ignore the more important things.
— Matt 23:23, Living New Testament

One of the reasons Jesus upset the Scribes and the Pharisees was that he was not a perfectionist. The Scribes and the Pharisees made their living, you see, serving a god who was made in their own perfectionist image and taught their perfectionist ways.

Probably one of their favorite passages in the Old Testament was the one in which the soldiers were carrying the Ark of the Covenant to safety. As they were hurrying along to flee the marauding enemies, the Ark tipped and began to fall. Uzzah reached out to steady it, and he was immediately struck by lightning. Why? Because Uzzah was not a Levite, and only Levites were allowed to touch the ark (2 Samuel 6:6–7).

The Scribes and the Pharisees also loved to catch people doing something wrong so they could have a party where someone got regularly stoned.

Men, women, children, and animals could get stoned if they violated one of the hundreds of existing religious laws at the time. No wonder Jesus got so furious with them—and they so furious with Him. The two camps were totally opposite in their approach to God—and godliness.

Jesus was not a perfectionist. He knew that every picnic would have its flies, and every person their flaws. He loved them anyway.

He was late to Mary and Martha's brother's bedside. He made it up to them later. He didn't care about washing dishes so much as renewing people's minds. He did not get hung up in minor details—like have the taxes been paid and do we have enough food for the people? He walked daily in the grace of his mission, and invited other people to do the same.

Perfectionists really won't get very far as spiritreneurs, because spiritreneurs have to learn to let go—to delegate—to fling their seeds upon the ground around them, even knowing not all of them will find root.

Spiritreneurs must let mistakes roll off their backs in order to keep moving forward. Intel has a process called "rolling implementation," which allows massive, multiple projects to progress, without assigning blame for failure. Yes, they've had failures, but these successes have changed our world.

In a news article about the genome factor, the story was told about a man who insisted that his company perfect the process for mapping each gene, while his competitors proceeded with the imperfect processes they had. The competitors ultimately got the lion's share of the profits, using "imperfect" processes.

An ancient proverb reads "An empty barn stays clean, but

there is no income from an empty barn." Flies will be present, but that's no reason to eliminate their cause, which is livestock. A horseman I confer with regularly told me that a university conducted a study where horses were raised in a fly-free barn. To their astonishment, the horses raised in a sterile atmosphere got sick more often than those raised with the normal amount of flies. Go figure.

Judy Moser, in her book, *Breaking the Chains of Perfectionism*, states that couples who have at least one perfectionist among them will eventually have major marital strife. Even a detail such as nagging a husband about putting too much milk in the oatmeal, or chastising a wife about the state of the linen closet, can be a tiny leak in a mighty ship that eventually runs aground.

Some people say, "The devil is in the details." I think that might be true—if the devil of details keeps you from seeing the big picture—if it keeps you from finishing that painting, or sending out the newsletters, or making that speech. . . .

The desire for perfectionism is a great excuse for staying stuck.

A friend of mine once told me that "many people say we are called to be perfect because Jesus said, 'You must be perfect, even as your Father in heaven is perfect.' "

The Hebrew translation of the word *perfect* is "compassionate." What an irony. The twist of a word leads to many twisted lives.

I recently went kayaking at Mission Bay with a land-loving friend of mine. Having kayaked for several years, I prided myself on doing it right. But this gal jumped in and with her double oar began slapping water all over the place. "Let me help you," I said. "No thank you," she said, "this is a great upper body workout!" So I sat there sulking and soaking as she labored inefficiently to get us to shore. "How many knots have we gone?" she shouted. "About five in my stomach so far!" I replied and then we burst out laughing. My way was no better than her way. And we both made it to shore.

Jesus was not a perfectionist.

Questions

1. Are you bound by the chains of perfectionism?
2. Do you keep polishing the silverware while your house is collapsing around you due to overall neglect?
3. Why can't spiritreneurs be perfectionists?
4. How many times are we supposed to forgive others' imperfections—even when they commit the same infraction over again?

Dear Lord,
Give me your adventurous, devil-may-care, compassionate courage in living. Let me leave my inner critic behind as I set sail daily with you, knowing that the salt in my face came from sea spray and daring, not from crying in my chair because of imperfectly cooked spaghetti.

Amen

HE ALLOWED ROOM
FOR CHILDREN

Let the children come unto me, for such is the king-dom of heaven.

—Matthew 18:2–6

A woman in one of our Path seminars shared that her eight-year-old adopted daughter from China was upset that she was not going to be able to accompany her mother to San Diego. Her mother said, "Honey, I'm sorry, but you can't come with me on this trip." Her daughter looked up at her with tear-filled eyes and said, "What—they don't allow children in California?"

We were all stirred by the poignancy of her belief—that an entire state could forbid entry to an entire class of people—little people, at that.

When Jesus said, "You must become like a child to enter the kingdom of heaven" (Luke 8:16), he meant that you must take on the mindset of a child—a mindset of simple and won-drous belief, a mindset of obedience, a mindset of willingness and desire to grow and learn.

It's as true in business as anywhere. We must allow room for the children among us—often disguised as adults—to grow and learn. And we must make room for growth within ourselves.

Hypocrites . . . brood of vipers . . . empty tombs . . . sons of Satan . . . are just a few choice phrases that Jesus applied to leaders who did not allow room for children—or growth—within their organization.

"One mistake and you're out of here, Carol," snarls her jealous supervisor. Who wants to work in an atmosphere where threats and the fear of failure are the only motivating force?

Spiritreneurs create, cultivate, and thrive in an atmosphere where learning, experimentation, excitement, and rapid forgiveness for mistakes are the norm, not the exception. It is a challenge and an invaluable discipline to determine that you are going to have a learning organization, rather than a perfect one.

One of my heroes is Ron, a brilliant businessman who loves developing people even more than businesses. At a recent meeting I was delighted to learn that his number two man in the organization started out as his chauffeur. Ron said, "Bob was my limo driver for several years. He was so willing to help out in every area of my life—whether it was changing diapers on my kids or picking them up from school. He proved to be so trustworthy with little things that I began to confide in him on trips. He used to sit right outside my door when I was having meetings, and finally I started inviting him in. He had such a wise, common-sense approach to complex business situations that I finally assigned him to head a small division within our company. He did so well with that he moved up to the top leadership levels of the firm, and today he sits here—a multimillionaire who I would trust with my life. In fact, come to think of it"—Ron laughed—"I have!"

Ron obviously allowed room for children in his organization—young fresh minds who were eager to learn new things. Ron saw beyond the chauffeur's cap to a fine mind waiting to be challenged, trusted, and trained.

Iconoclast CEO Leland Boren tells the joke that he hired an engineer fresh out of school to work in one of his manufacturing plants. When the young man showed up for duty Leland handed him a broom and said, "Your first task is to sweep out the plant." The young man stood there sputtering in anger. "But sir, I have a Ph.D.!" "Oh, that's right, I forgot!" Leland said apologetically, taking back the broom. "Here—let me show you how it's done," Leland said, demonstrating his best broom-sweep technique, as well as the fact that the young man had just entered a learning organization.

When Jesus recruited his team they *all* had to be retrained. Those who were willing to be trained, flourished. Those who were not willing, failed. Jesus did not just see his team as who they appeared to be, or what their former job descriptions were—he saw in them the willingness to learn.

Spiritreneurs must think the same way. We must treat it all as an experiment, not a life-or-death game. The joy will be what we learn and master along the way—not what we came in knowing.

One company I know refers to itself as "an organism" rather than an organization. They have a motto that reads, "No shame—no blame." When a problem or slipup occurs, the team is committed to finding out why it happened and then immediately work to see that it doesn't happen again. Their focus is on the future, not what happened yesterday or last week. Knowing that there will be no lasting grudges or re-criminations helps all of them put their weight fully to the plow, rather than standing around slapping each other silly for oversights or mistakes.

Jesus had the same kind of organism going—no shame, no blame—just acknowledge what went wrong and then fix it.

Thank God Peter was in a learning environment. He would have not lasted thirty days in a perfectionist environment—or perhaps even in most churches today—yet he became a pillar of courage, of vision, of faithfulness, built upon the foundation of all the mistakes he had made before.

Jesus allowed room for children.

Questions

1. Do you currently work in a learning environment or a "you should have known" environment?
2. If it is not a learning environment, what specific steps could you take to create one?
3. Where or when have you been in a learning organism like Jesus created? What were the characteristics?
4. Why is having a learning environment vital for spiritreneurs?

Dear Lord,
Your name meant teacher as well as savior. Help me be a willing, open, and joyous student. And help me treat others with the same faith, respect, and trust you have given me.

Amen

HE EXPERIENCED
TRANSFIGURATION

And he was transfigured before them.
    —Matthew 17:2

We know that Jesus wept, sweat, and bled. He could manifest extraordinary things externally, but there is one particular moment when he experienced transfiguration.

"Six days later Jesus took with him Peter and James and his brother John and led them up a high mountain by themselves. There in their presence he was transfigured: his face shone like the sun and his clothes became as dazzling as light. And suddenly Moses and Elijah appeared to them; they were talking with him" (Matthew 17:1–3). His body was so ringed with light that he became almost invisible. The change was so unusual and moving to his disciples that they wanted to erect a monument to commemorate the moment.

I can't help but wonder what caused that transfiguration. I used to think that it was God throwing a spotlight on His precious son to help the clueless disciples get a glimpse of who they were dealing with. But after becoming a spiritreneur, I'm beginning to think that perhaps Jesus experienced transfiguration at that particular moment because he was doing what he most loved—conversing with Moses and Elijah, two prophets he had long studied, and being in the presence of coworkers he loved.

. When you are doing what you most love, in the presence of the people who love and believe in you, you too can experience an incredible lightness of being—a transparency of your soul. This is the daily divine connection, which is the privilege and joy of those who allow God to flow freely through them in their work.

Moses, who was said to be a friend of God, also experienced a form of transfiguration when he spent time communing with God on Mount Sinai. The result of this spiritual retreat was that "when Moses came down from Mount Sinai . . . the skin of his face was radiant because he had been talking to God. Aaron and the Israelites were afraid to go near him because his skin was so radiant" (Exodus 34:29–30). Moses, spiritreneur, was experiencing the transfiguring power of God by allowing God to flow through him as he did his work.

This, ultimately, is what spiritreneurs are called to do—to let God's love flow through us as we do our daily work. Lately I've been meditating on Jesus' "I Am" statements. When he said, "I am the way"—he was, in a sense, saying that he was opening himself up so people could see God—and come to God—through him. Are we not called to do the same? To love in such a way that people can look through us and see God—not just on Saturday or Sunday, but on Monday and Tuesday too?

Transfiguration is happening in El Paso, Texas, as a businessman pours himself into, through, and beyond his highly successful company. George F. Cudahy, owner of American Eagle Brick Company, says he benefitted as a child from "encouragers and beacons of hope" in his life. Last year he began to mentor ten at-risk children in El Paso, meeting with them twice a month. They all carry a card with his telephone number on it. Cudahy talks with each student about what he or she is doing, and then the students talk about career paths where they might employ their gifts.

Thirteen-year-old Edward Ibanez shyly shared that he'd always dreamed of flying. When Cudahy promised to take him for an airplane ride, Edward didn't believe him. Yet two months later Edward was sitting in the pilot's seat of a glider—flying with a friend of Cudahy's at the West Texas Airport. "It happened!" exclaimed an exuberant Edward. "I learned that it is possible to achieve your dreams. Now I want to become a pilot in the air force."

Laura Herrera expressed an interest in being a pediatrician. Cudahy arranged for her to shadow Dr. Kim Rodriguez at her office for three hours. Margaret Garcia told Cudahy she likes to take care of animals. Now she shadows a local veterinarian. Juan Solis was unsure about his career path. His love of radios led Cudahy to get him a crystal radio set to assemble. Now Juan foresees a future in electronics.

Transfigured lives. Vague, cloudy dreams transfigured into positive, crystal-clear goals. George F. Cudahy, a man who owns a brick company, is laying foundations in human souls which will last through eternity. He has opened himself up to allow God to flow through him. Cudahy is a spiritreneur who has experienced transfiguration.

Perhaps you, too, have had moments in your work where you felt ringed with light and unaware of time. As we each allow God to pour through us, we are becoming transfigured.

Jesus experienced transfiguration.

Questions

1. Have you ever experienced a form of transfiguration in your work, in your life? When was it? Who was with you? What were you doing? Describe the feeling and the memory in detail.
2. If you haven't experienced transfiguration, would you like to?
3. How would you advise someone who wants to experience Divine Connection on a daily basis—during working hours, too?
4. How can you create a schedule and/or environment where transfiguration is almost a daily event?

Dear Lord,

We are so much more than we seem to be. Help me remember to make the time to climb the mountain with you. Let me be the friend you talk to as we look out on the valley. Let me breathe in daily your intoxicating love, and pour it out through my being.

Amen

HE GAVE IT AWAY

Freely ye have received, freely give.
　　　　　　　　　—Matthew 10:8

Many of the people who now run thriving enterprises found that the first rung of the ladder to success was not marked with instant profits but with an immediate depletion of inventory.

Debbie Fields of Mrs. Fields' Cookies did not have an easy time getting people to come up to her counter. So, she broke up the cookies into bite-size samples and began giving them away. One little taste was all it took to get the people hooked. By first giving away what she had she launched a multimillion-dollar empire.

Scripture clearly states that the *first fruits* belong to God—not the leftovers. For some reason it is vital that we take the first and best of what we have and release it—release it as an offering . . . a sacrifice . . . a thank you. Release it so that we acknowledge and remember our source. Release it so that there is now an opening into which God's good can flow. Kahlil Gibran wrote that "the fear of thirst is the thirst that can never be quenched." By giving away the best of what we have, we have conquered our fear of thirst. And thus we will be satisfied.

Just recently I had a telephone consultation with a young woman who earned $200,000 last year. One of the reasons she called me is because she has lost her passion for her work. The other reason is because she is terrified of being unable to pay the bills—not next year's, next month's. I realized that this woman was so afraid of loss because she could not give and she was shriveling up inside. My "prescription" for her included volunteering at a shelter for battered women one night a week.

Three weeks later she called me to say that she had taken her eight- and ten-year-old sons with her so they could play with the other children there. As she sat and listened to the stories of women who had given up everything just so they and their children could be safe, she began to realize how fortunate she was. Her sons, shocked to learn that there were actually children who had no toys, began a toy drive at their school. Those three hours a week she gave away made her feel more fulfilled and "abundant" than any amount of time she could have spent trying to fill a bank account that would before never have been enough. Sheryl got rich by giving something away.

This concept also works in terms of customer service. One of my favorite stories to illustrate this point is that of two little girls who opened up a refreshment stand on a busy corner in Atlanta. A businessman drove up and was amazed by their sign. It read "Ice Cold Water." He took a glass and gulped it down and asked the girl who gave it to him, "How much do I owe you?" She smiled. "Nothing! It's free." With that he took out a dollar bill and put it in her hand. As he was getting back into his car he heard the girl exult to her friend, "That makes forty-four dollars we've made so far!" Not a bad return on something they were giving away.

Nipun Mehta and his band of friends are like many other young intellects starting IPOs in Silicon Valley, yet their goal is not getting rich but giving away their technological skills to help bring nonprofit agencies up to speed. Airline Ambassadors in Burlingame was one of the first beneficiaries of Nipun's Company, Charity Focus.

The three-year-old airline program, which exists solely on donations, provides free travel and escorts for orphans and sick children around the world. Thanks to Nipun and his friends, the program will now save thousands of dollars normally spent on marketing outreach. Nipun, like the other volunteers, works at Charity Focus on his own time, often after pulling long shifts at his regular job as a computer programmer. He holds his hands like two pans on a scale. "Sleep a little longer, or help somebody else." He smiles as he says, "You can't even compare the two." Nipun and the seventy-plus volunteers at Charity Focus are getting rich, truly rich, by giving it away.

If you really believe in your product or service, then you won't hesitate to give some of it away. The goodwill and customer loyalty you can build through this approach is endless. One young Internet company built a customer base of ten million subscribers in less than a year—by giving their service away. The founders, all students in their twenties, admitted that they had a hard time finding backers when their business plan read "Give it away" and their sales income column read "Zero." However, these kids were onto something, because three years later they sold their company to a bigger Internet company for one hundred million dollars. Apparently the powers at the top realized that a ten million–member subscriber base was worth a lot of money.

Proverbs states that people who water others will be watered themselves. People who hoard what they have will be punished.

The Dead Sea is dead because it has no outlets. Whatever flows into it never leaves. Have you met people like that? Have you dealt with companies like that? And though they may wring every last ounce of energy or nickel out of you, they are left with a depleted and demoralized customer. Is it worth it to save a dollar and lose a hundred? To lock up everything you own so tightly that nothing will escape?

The *G* in God stands for generosity. If we are to be like God—experience God—and commune with God, *generosity* must be one of the first words people use to describe us.

Remember, the only plant Jesus ever cursed was the fig tree that refused to share its fruit with a very hungry, very powerful, and very giving-oriented man.

Break yourself like the bread, and you will be multiplied. Pour yourself out like wine, and you too will enjoy the party—especially since your generosity will guarantee you a seat next to God.

Jesus gave it away.

Questions

1. What do you have that you could give away, in terms of your time? your possessions? your products? your services?
2. When will you do so?
3. Do you give your first fruits to God—or scrape off the leftovers?
4. Why is giving such an integral part of receiving?

Dear Lord,
Teach me to give—to release—to share—the very best of what I have without expectation of return. All I am and have is yours. Let me hold things lightly, lest they turn around and choke the life out of me. May I never fear thirst, because I always give my first cup of water away.

Amen

HE EMBRACED THE PRESENCE
OF GOD

The upright shall dwell in thy presence.
—Psalms 140:13

Recently I got a phone call from a former minister, now a highly paid corporate consultant. He called me because he was struggling with his newfound success. Never expecting or even seeking money as a goal, he now finds himself being sought after by CEOs who are willing to pay many thousands of dollars for his services. Ironically, he was fired by his small-town congregation for being too advanced in his thinking. He remembers curling up in the fetal position right by the altar the night the board asked him to leave. "I thought I was going to die from the pain," he said slowly. "Yet that was the night I was set free." So now here he is, prospering.

"I'm calling you because I want a reality check," he said. "I'm doing all this consulting work, and I love it. But I still want to talk about God. For me, the presence of God is the only reality I've ever known. I want to talk about that with rabbis and non-churchgoers and anyone else who might view Christianity from a different perspective. To me, the essence of Christianity is the presence of God."

Greg's words have really made me think about the joyous privilege we have, yet so often forget, which is to be in the presence of God. Another friend of mine, who runs women's retreats in Montana, did a workshop recently where she told the participants this: "Don't visualize what you want out of the next three to five years. Visualize what you want in this moment." As I read her words, I realized that all my planning and visualizing the future so easily takes me away from what I really want, which is to be in the presence of God. And that I can have instantly—if I will only ask.

I have long contended that the reason the disciples and apostles and saints and martyrs were willing to be tortured and beaten and maimed and destroyed was not due to their fear of hell—but to their overwhelming desire to be in Christ's presence again.

As I write these words well after midnight on a moonlit night, I am thinking about the concept of presence—the times when I have felt Jesus so close to me . . . and times when others have brought him to me in the form of loving communion.

I am reminded of the train trip my friend Linda and I took to Europe last fall. We entered into a private coach on the train going from Venice to Vienna. Having known each other since we were teenagers, there is the comfort of shared histories and common laughter that makes it so easy to be together. Since we have been separated by physical distance for most of our friendship, we were delighted to have uninterrupted time just to talk, dream, cry, and wonder together. As we settled into our coach, the train began its gentle climb through the Italian Alps. The sun was setting, and in the green field below us we could hear the church bells signaling the end of the day. Out the window I could see the train's powerful locomotive engine curling around the mountain, its picturesque puffs of gray smoke adding to the low-lying clouds. The train rocked us with its gentle rhythm, and, in awe of the beauty around us, the two of us spoke not a word. Finally I said, "Linda, I am sure that this is how the Lord takes people to heaven." She smiled and gently patted my feet, which were propped up comfortably on the seat beside her.

For hours we rode into the dark, in silence. Oh, the indescribable joy of being in the presence of someone who knows you and loves you even though you shrank her blouse and used the rent money to buy flowers. I flew to Linda after my divorce and she flew to me when my father died. Such a presence of Christ and his unconditional love this longtime friend brings to me.

Another time I felt Christ's presence was when I was doing a late-night book-signing in Atlanta. Book tours are long, arduous events which humorist Dave Barry aptly asserts are "designed to kill authors." I was exhausted and on the verge of being really cranky. Grateful for the people who had gathered to get their books signed, I was still asking myself why I was doing this when I could be home playing with my horses, until I looked up and saw him. He was standing by one of the pillars—wearing blue jeans and brown loafers. His head was tilted and he looked at me with a grin so full of love and recognition and knowing that my heart literally leaped within me. Jesus was with me on my tour.

I sense him everywhere, don't you? Like this morning when Little Pistol, my newborn sorrel filly, began leaping and cavorting, testing her one-week-old legs. As graceful as a ballerina, as full of fire as a jalapeño pepper, this little filly took my breath away with her newfound joy at being alive. And I felt his presence there with me—watching her with a heart so full it almost felt like bursting.

I also felt the presence of Christ at a funeral. My friend's mother had died of Alzheimer's. When my friend walked up to the casket and began caressing her mother's face, I couldn't keep from sobbing. As I began to weep very loudly, I felt it. The presence of God. The congregation had begun chanting. "Hail Mary, full of grace. The Lord is with thee. Blessed is the fruit of thy womb Jesus. Pray for us now, and in the hour of our death." And then, without even pausing for a breath, the group began the chant again. "Hail Mary, full of grace. The Lord is with thee . . ." The group prayer wrapped itself around me and calmed me down as a daughter caressed her mother's face for the very last time. In those common, beautiful words I felt the presence of Christ. "Hail, Mary, full of grace. The Lord is with thee."

Last week a fourteen-year-old boy was killed one block from my home. He was riding his new motorbike, which slid out of control and hit a tree. He died instantly. The only son of an older couple. Gone. I walked outside my door yesterday and found two baby birds that had been swept out of the tree. Fierce forty-mile-an-hour winds had shaken trees and buildings the night before, and these two baby birds, about to get their feathers, lay dead at my feet. Every single day in this world, parents' hearts are broken. There are no words to explain or comfort. I only know that God knows and sees. The Lord is near to the brokenhearted. How I long for the presence of God to fill their hearts—the mother bird who lost her babies, and the mother who lost her only son on a bright and beautiful afternoon.

I think about the presence of Christ as the man hands me my change. I have purchased another treasure find from a junk furniture shop, and I am so excited about showing it to Mom that I almost forget to notice him. He asks me what I do and I say casually I am a writer. He asks me what I write about and I say, "Spirituality." I reach for the cord that is going to secure my newfound purchase to the truck bed for the ride home. He steps up to me and asks more. "Do you work with individuals?" I am in such a hurry to leave that I start to say, "Not really," and then I realize what transaction is taking place. To practice the presence of Christ means putting down your purchase and looking into the eyes of the vendor who sold it to you, to see what is in his soul, not just what is in his store.

Spiritreneurs embrace and practice the presence of God. That is why we are here. "Behold, I am with you always" (Matthew 28:20).

Jesus embraced the presence of God.

Questions

1. Do you embrace and practice the presence of God in your business? When? How?

2. When have you experienced the presence of God?

3. Who else brings you the presence of God through their loving communion with you?

4. Have you told them what they bring you—in ways they can understand?

5. How might you bring the presence of God into your work more?

Dear Lord,

Be with me now. Stay with me always. May I feel your heartbeat beside me constantly.

Amen

HE SAID, "DAYENU"

D*ayenu* (die ay´ new) is a Hebrew word which means "it is enough," or "that would have been enough." At the Passover supper, religious Jews repeat phrases like this:

> *If God had delivered us from Egypt,*
> *and not given us the Torah,*
> Dayenu.
> *If God had given us the Torah,*
> *and not taken us to Israel,*
> Dayenu.
> Dayenu. *It would have been enough.*

This word is vital to spiritreneurs, for we have a tendency to never say "enough." There is a discontent and restlessness within us that drives us ever onward, which, if not brought into balance, can lead to our spiritual, moral, and financial ruin.

The CEO whose mergers and media triumphs have tripled the stock price, yet still cannot sleep because of a rival's outstanding success, needs the word *dayenu*.

If David had said *dayenu* with his first wife, he would never have pursued Bathsheba—a sin that cost him his dignity and became a blot on his legacy.

How much is enough?

The inability or unwillingness to answer this question is a great cause of our discontent. How many shoes, or cars, or houses does one person really need?

Dayenu is not about limits, it is about fullness—about recognizing and counting the blessings we have, right there, in the moment.

Ahh. To be able to say *dayenu*—that is wealth.

I remember taking Tara, my five-year-old niece, to Sea World. As we watched the otters twirl and play, she pointed gleefully to one that had rolled over on its back and was patting an abalone shell on its stomach.

"Look, Aunt Laurie. He's saying 'I'm rich!' " She laughed. Indeed, the creature was saying *dayenu*.

I have learned to interpret my horses' snorts. There is the snort of anger and defiance—as when my two stallions meet at the gate. There is the snort of anticipation as I wheel out the grain to feed them in their stalls. But my favorite snort is the one when we are riding on the trail. Perhaps the sun is just going down and the crickets are starting up their songs. The dogs are bounding alongside in the alfalfa fields and my horse, Miss Velvet, lets out a snort of pure contentment—the joy of being in motion and feeling our bodies move in rhythm on a beautiful day. I know that snort well. It says to me *dayenu . . .* this is what living is about.

Yet so many businesspeople I know never snort happily *dayenu.* Their quest is ever on the horizon, over the hill, eluding them. One million is not enough anymore. It's got to be two or ten or twelve.

I know an executive who founded and owns a company where revenues last year topped $26 million. Bill wants to sell the company and pursue his passion for motivational speaking. Susan, his wife, refuses to let him consider this line of thinking. She stops him cold with, "How can you make money at that?"

I have to wonder, as I did with him recently, why he couldn't comfortably retire at the age of forty-six on $26 million or so and speak for free if he wanted to for the rest of his life. Susan doesn't see it that way. *Dayenu* is, unfortunately, not in her vocabulary.

The *dayenu* principle was poignantly demonstrated to me when the six-year-old son of a close family friend was hit by a car while chasing a ball into the street. The boy lingered in a coma for months, with doctors offering little hope of recovery. Prayer teams from churches all around moved in to support the family in a twenty-four-hour circle of prayer. Finally, after three months, the boy's father said, "I know what I must do." While the mother looked on he took the child in his arms, and lifted his tiny body up.

"Dear God," he choked out, "you have given us six wonderful years with your son Jonathan. He was always yours. You just loaned him to us for a season. And if six years is all he was destined to have, then it is enough. We release him back to you. Your will be done."

Within minutes the boy's spirit slipped away, and he went back to God. The father said *dayenu.*

Do you ever say *dayenu?* Can you shut the engines off for a while to listen to the crickets? Can you count each receipt with gratitude and say, "The manna was good again today. Just enough. Just right." Can you see the smile on your child's face as she runs leaping into your arms and says, "Daddy, I've missed you. Come see the surprises I have."

I try to surround myself with *dayenu* people—filled with *dayenu* moments. Children are very much like that. So are animals. The Hispanic culture with its emphasis on piñata parties and eloquent masses and every saint having a feast day—every plan sealed with "God willing," even if it is just for a lunch gathering, seem to understand *Dayenu.* Perhaps that's why I live in two border cities, cities saturated with a culture of values in family and friendships rather than what kind of car you drive.

Recently Dee, my administrator, was firing off details of our mutual itineraries—her trip to Mexico to seal a licensing deal, my invitation to the coronation of a king in Ghana, Africa. On top of the pile was a letter from the lieutenant governor of Texas who had just read *Jesus, CEO* and wanted to get together. We were discussing the scholarship details of the next Path seminar, and suddenly I took her hand and said, "*Dayenu.*"

She looked up at me slowly and said, "Yes, Laurie. *Dayenu.*" If only God had given us this, it would have been enough.

Maybe Jesus said *dayenu* while walking through a meadow and pausing to look at a newborn lamb. Maybe he said it as a youth, holding up a finely polished piece of wood. Maybe he said it as he lifted a baby bird back into its nest. Even from the cross, Jesus said, "Into your hands I commit my spirit. It is enough."

Jesus said, "*Dayenu.*"

Questions

1. What are your *dayenu* moments?
2. When was the last time you had one? Describe it in detail. Remember and share the feeling.
3. Under stress, can a *dayenu* moment shift the perception from defeat to victory?
4. What does it take to have a *dayenu?*
5. How many can you have?
6. How many does God have? How many with you?

Oh Lord,
You know the desires and ambitions and fears in my heart, which so often lead to stress and anxiety. Help me recall in detail every gift and blessing you've given me, so that I can rest with you—and hear the crickets call rather than the cannons, and say dayenu—*even this would be enough.*
Amen

HE WALKED IN BEAUTY

*How beautiful on the mountains are the feet of those
who bring good news.*

—Isaiah 52:7

Jesus walked in beauty. Perhaps that is what helped him
balance huge spiritual and emotional demands. He went
into a garden to pray. He walked through fields of lilies and
contemplated their wardrobe. He felt if he could remind us to
walk in beauty too, perhaps we wouldn't stress out so much
over daily details.

"See how the lilies of the field grow. They do not labor or
spin. Yet I tell you that not even Solomon in all his splendor
was dressed like one of these" (Matthew 28:29).

My friend Catherine stunned me several years ago with a
personal observation. We were walking through the desert
hills of Santa Teresa, New Mexico. I was detailing to her how
my rental properties were doing (well) and then began to lay
out the expansion plans for the business, when she said,
"Laurie, I think you are a sensual illiterate."

"What?" I gasped. I've never been called illiterate in my life—until now.

She said, "How much time did you spend eating lunch today?"

"Ten minutes," I replied.

"What did you eat yesterday for dinner?" she continued.

"I don't remember."

"When was the last time you had a pedicure?"

"Never!" I exclaimed. "I hate people touching my feet."

She smiled. "When was the last time you took a one-hour bubble bath?"

"Baths? Who has time for baths? I dash in and out of the shower."

She stopped. "What do you smell out here in the desert?"

I stopped and had to confess, "Nothing."

"Do I make my point?" she asked.

"Yes," I said sadly. "I am a Sensual Illiterate." Or should I say—was. I have embarked on a serious recovery program that includes lighting candles, having regular massages, and chewing and recognizing my food—savoring it, actually. I still have a long way to go.

You see, I am a spiritreneur, and the last half of that word still tends to dominate. My idea of a vacation is spending two hours at Office Depot, lingering on each aisle, trying out every desk, sampling the office chairs, caressing file folders and spiral binders. I have a collection of organizers, calendars, calculators, and briefcases that now almost rivals that of the store itself. Yet I know that in order to keep a balance I must spend time in nature. I must reconnect with my senses—taste, touch, hearing, smell, and seeing most of all. I find that as I collect those little moments of "sensing" that I create a necklace of peaceful memories that I can take into any boardroom.

One of my favorite sensing activities now is feeding my goldfish in the large brick pond in my backyard. I planted water lilies in it this summer, and now their delicate yellow blooms enchant me as their smooth green pads reach out across the water. When I first planted them I was surprised to see the goldfish swim across the stems, sensually brushing their bodies against the giving fronds. Their swishing sound as they circle around to swim over the stems yet again delights me. I now have sixty-two very happy fish out there. I meet with them regularly, just to watch them in graceful motion.

Author Sarah Ban Breathnach has made a career out of writing books that can help anyone, especially women, contemplate their own beauty, as well as that around them. Oprah said Sarah's advice to keep a daily gratitude journal was the single most life-changing exercise she's ever done. When we begin to say thank you is when we begin to see the beauty around us.

I stood last night in the barn with my white Arabian stallion. It was raining outside and the rain on the tin roof was like a gentle symphony. He smelled my neck and then rested his head on my shoulder. I turned to really look at him—his head with the dark eyes so full and searching, as Catherine says, "exuding his soul," the veins running from his powerful jaw down to his delicate nose, the white forelock of hair gracefully cascading down his forehead. . . . We looked at each other for a few long, beautiful moments. "This is what it's all about," I thought. "Beauty—after all."

This Navajo prayer is one every spiritreneur might be wise to pray, and remember:

In beauty may I walk
all day long may I walk
through the returning seasons
may I walk
beautifully will I possess again
beautiful birds
beautiful, joyful birds.
On the trail marked with pollen
May I walk
with grasshoppers about my feet
May I walk
with the dew about my feet
May I walk
with beauty before me, behind me,
above me, all around me
May I walk
In old age wandering on a
trail of beauty lively,
May I walk.
It is finished in beauty.
It is finished in beauty.

Jesus walked in beauty.

Questions

1. Are you a sensual illiterate?
2. Have you neglected and abandoned your senses just to hang out in your mind?
3. What did you smell today—touch today—taste today—hear today—see, really see today?
4. Do you keep a gratitude journal? If so, is it filled with beauty?

Dear Lord,
You created me with such highly refined and sophisticated senses—help me use and appreciate them more. Help me not be a sensual illiterate on my quest to success, for only when I walk in beauty can I really walk with you.

Amen

EPILOGUE

A nyone linking Jesus to business is in danger, at first glance, of contributing to the same mismessaging that caused him to overturn the money-changers tables in the temple. "My Father's house is a house of prayer," he cried, "yet you have made it a den of thieves" (Matthew 21:13).

Spiritreneurs do not set out to harness God in order to make more money. Rather, spiritreneurs allow God to harness them, and in so doing experience glory. This book has ultimately been about the process of surrender—the joy, the terror, the chaos, and calm that comes from stepping into the unknown and allowing God's breath to breathe through you.

In reading the Gospels again last night I was struck by the passage when Jesus met with the apostles for the last time. They had gathered in the Upper Room, and were overjoyed to see him. After speaking with them for a few moments, it says "He breathed on them" (John 20:22).

He did not brand them. He did not hand them maps, or whips, or chains, or even time cards. He gave them a new breath of the spirit that is Holy, and they were never the same.

Each of those people in that room became a spiritreneur—dedicating their lives to him, supporting and being supported as they lived out their new missions. In the television miniseries *Jesus,* Jesus says to his disciples at one point, "Your mission begins on earth, and ends in eternity." This is what spiritreneurs understand. We begin to build here and now with the talents we have been given, working on a foundation that will endure into eternity.

We live now in unusual times. We have tools at our disposal that allow us to work with anyone in the world, anywhere in the world, twenty-four hours a day. We are amassing wealth and information at speeds never before thought possible.

Yet are we increasing in wisdom? Are we experiencing the peace Jesus spoke about "that passes understanding"? And perhaps most important of all, how are we treating "the least of these my brethren"?

These three questions are in the minds and hearts of every true spiritreneur. We can do well by doing right and thereby enjoy true success. My prayer is that we each shall hear those beautiful words: "Well done, my good and faithful servant. In you I am well pleased."

Ultimately, the spiritreneur's guide can be found in these few words: "Seek first the kingdom of heaven, and all else will be given to you."

ABOUT THE AUTHOR

Laurie Beth Jones is the author of the national bestsellers *Jesus, CEO: Using Ancient Wisdom for Visionary Leadership; The Path: Creating Your Mission for Work and Life;* and *Jesus in Blue Jeans.*

After launching and running her own successful advertising agency for fifteen years, Laurie Beth Jones burst onto the national scene with *Jesus, CEO.* Using practical wisdom, humor, and reality-based thinking, Ms. Jones has become one of the world's leading consultants for businesses that want to take their work, and their workers, to unparalleled levels of performance, satisfaction, and success.

Her work has reached places as high as the White House, the Pentagon, the halls of Congress and the Senate, as well as workers in the streets of Calcutta, Bosnia, and South Africa. She lives out her mission daily, which is to "recognize, promote, and inspire the divine connection in myself and others."

CONTACT INFORMATION

If you would like to know more about our Path training seminars, the free Jesus CEO University on-line course, our corporate speaking and consulting services, offerings for children, and other current information, check out our website at lauriebethjones.com or jesusceo.com.

Contact address is:

The Jones Group
609 E. Blacker Ave.
El Paso, Texas 79902
phone: 915-541-6033
fax: 915-541-6034